STUDIO WORKS 6

Harvard University Graduate School of Design

Editors

Darell Fields
Associate Professor of Architecture

Brooke Hodge
Director of Lectures, Exhibitions,
and Academic Publications

Student Editors

Nicholas Tobier
MLA '00

Hunter Tura
MArch '00

Dean, Faculty of Design

Peter G. Rowe

International Standard Serial Number

1060-8486

Published by Harvard University Graduate
School of Design

Distributed in the United States of America
by Princeton Architectural Press

Printed in the United States of America

Copies of *Studio Works 6* are available for
purchase from:

Harvard University
Graduate School of Design
Book Orders
48 Quincy Street
Cambridge, MA 02138
617.496.5113

http://st1.yahoo.com/harvarddesignbooks/

Dean's Prologue

As in the past, the aim of this issue of *Studio Works* is to capture the essential character of the design studio experience at the Graduate School of Design. In short, it provides both an overview and vignettes of a year in the life of design students at Harvard, and an archive of their design speculations and deliberations. This year's theme involves not only presenting current work but also finding links back into the Design School's institutional past. In the pages that follow you will find excerpts from that past, along with contemporary commentary and comparisons between now and then.

For substantial periods of this century, design education has been concerned explicitly with new ideas, novel developments, and with what is sometimes now referred to as the 'cutting edge' of its various sub-disciplines. Indeed, one might even argue that high-quality education, in and of itself, must embody a significant appreciation of new developments, if the knowledge and know-how conveyed is to remain current and relevant. On the other hand, the terrain of the intellectual past is often turned toward for experience, tried-and-true practices, and ways of making things that have stood the test of time. Therefore, invariably a tension exists in most pedagogical schemes between conveying well-known and often time-honored principles together with excursions along the frontiers of knowledge and, in the case of design, taste and practice as well. The equation between old and new is also further complicated in institutional settings like the Design School by the pedagogical and related history of the place itself. By now it is well-known that many ideas about modern architecture and modern design, for instance, made their way to the United States from Europe via the Graduate School of Design during the middle to late 1930s. This importation clearly changed the way design would be considered and taught throughout the country but also how it would be taught here at the Design School during subsequent generations. We are, as it were, at once the beneficiaries and occasional victims of our own institutional histories, quite apart from how we might reflect and project ourselves with regard to the outside world. Just how these influences can be traced in the studio work of the School is one of the central themes of this issue.

Regardless of differences in format, all studios have a specific pedagogical focus, although no attempt is made to comprehensively simulate office practice. Rather, all studios operate within a thematic framework with specific educational, as distinct from strictly professional, objectives. To make an analogy with certain ideas from other disciplines, the explicitly exploratory nature of design studios makes them rather more speculative than simply normal or routine in their focal interests—returning again to the idea of the 'new.' Here advantage is also taken of a strong and broadly-based program of visiting critics—another hallmark of the studio experience at the Graduate School of Design. These advantages include an added breadth of perspective, different styles of studio instruction, and a widened design outlook on the part of participants.

Peter G. Rowe
Dean, Faculty of Design

Introduction to the Departments

Architecture

For generations, Harvard has educated committed men and women who have assumed major leadership roles in shaping the built environment. Today's graduates in architecture continue this tradition by answering the demanding challenges posed by contemporary society. Architects draw upon knowledge and experience gained from the past while adapting to the changing needs of the modern world. Some roles played by the architect remain the same, but new ways of thinking in the profession have emerged; the school remains vigilant to this evolution, understanding that the demands on design grow increasingly complex and require new interpretations.

The selection of work by students in the Department of Architecture, shown in *Studio Works 6,* represents the varied pedagogical objectives of the department's sequential studio structure. Each studio experience—from core studios to studio options and, finally, to the independent design thesis—is an opportunity for the distillation and synthesis of the complex and far-reaching issues that define architecture.

The four-semester-long core sequence progresses from the design of small projects with limited scope and narrowly focused objectives through larger and more complex projects with ambitious urban intentions that engage, through architecture, a broad range of sociocultural and physical concerns. The studio options, offered in conjunction with those of the Departments of Landscape Architecture and Urban Planning and Design, provide students with the opportunity to explore architecture through a diversity of issues, scales, technologies, and critical positions. The thesis program, in which each student works with an advisor from the faculty, promotes and enables significant individual and independent research in design. At all levels of studio instruction, the pedagogic programs provide students and faculty with an open-ended discourse about the possibilities of contemporary architecture.

It is the commitment of the Department of Architecture to focus our academic and pedagogical agendas on the larger and interconnected social, cultural, and technological issues that architecture must always engage.

Jorge Silvetti, *Chair*
Nelson Robinson, Jr., Professor of Architecture

Urban Planning and Design

The department of Urban Planning and Design brings together scholars and professionals who address the critical and complex conditions of modern cities and towns. In addition to design, faculty specialties and courses of instruction encompass legal, socioeconomic, environmental, historical, and aesthetic influences on urban planning and design. Students in the urban planning and design programs address problems of increasing development in the suburbs, the decaying structure of older cities, and the responsibility for shaping future development to meet social, economic, and cultural needs, while preserving and enhancing those aspects of urban form that have enduring value. In mastering the roles of urban planners and designers, GSD students learn to apply their knowledge of social values and historic precedents, along with their design skills, to urban conditions. Particular emphasis is placed on inquiry, speculation, and practice through design studio offerings and the pursuit of individual thesis projects.

The studio sequence begins with Elements of Urban Design and Planning, a core offering required of all incoming students in urban design and urban planning. Three semesters of option studios follow. Collectively, they are a key component in the professional training of planners and designers and allow students to develop their problem solving skills by exploring a range of urban interventions.

The studio options offered each term address theoretical and pragmatic issues pertinent to the planning and design of cities in the US and abroad. They offer an opportunity to explore a range of public and private interventions in different cultural contexts. The combination of domestic and foreign locations provides an invaluable tool to compare urban revitalization issues common to cities, and to distinguish the economic, social and institutional factors that are unique to the site and influence the search for an appropriate planning and physical design solution. Studios sponsored by donors allow field trips to the sites. This year, students traveled to Bilbao, Spain; Cleveland; Denver; New York; Rome; and Singapore.

The independent thesis gives students an opportunity to explore topics of their own interest. These topics vary in scope and include design demonstrations of urban design principles and concepts, abstract design explorations into theoretical issues of interest, and academic studies of a theoretical or historical nature.

François Vigier, *Chair*
Charles Dyer Norton Professor of Regional Planning

Landscape Architecture

For a full one hundred years, Harvard's teaching in landscape architecture has prepared men and women for professional activities in all pursuits related to land—land as the place of inhabitation, as resource, as the place of production or construction, as infrastructure, as commodity, and as the site of artistic engagement. The works of landscape architecture vary in scale and scope, ranging from the garden and the community to large tracts of land and regional systems. As urbanization worldwide continues to produce change in the land, landscape architects increasingly strive to keep the concerns of ecology and natural systems in the foreground of design and planning.

At Harvard the design studio is the center of inquiry and research. Knowledge gained in coursework in history, theory, technology, visual studies, and the sciences is critically fused to the work in the studio, so that the first four semesters—which constitute the core program—are intended to be synthetic and cumulative. Studio projects in the first semester begin with limited scope and narrowly-defined pedagogical objectives. Scale and complexity increase each semester, such that by the third and fourth semesters, projects confront issues of community, infrastructure, and landscape systems in complicated urban or urbanizing conditions. Beyond the core program, the option level studios offer the student varied and focused opportunities to engage advanced studio topics inside the department as well as with faculty and colleagues in the departments of Architecture and Urban Planning and Design.

The Department of Landscape Architecture recognizes and embraces an expanding discourse concerning landscape culture, and it is our intention to capitalize on its enlarged place in academic inquiry and in building practices. Every day the world's populations realize the increasingly critical imperative to take account of the landscape, to understand its dynamic workings, to ensure its survival—and to retain its pervasive role in the formation of culture itself.

George Hargreaves, *Chair*
Professor in Practice of Landscape Architecture

in this issue:

summer, 1941, fifty cents a copy

TASK, A MAGAZINE FOR THE YOUNGER GENERATION IN ARCHITECTURE. Cambridge, 1941–1948. (Rare Periodical)

Editorial Statement

Studio Works 6 is the first of the GSD's series of student work publications to position the present pedagogy of the school in relation to its now mythologized past. By considering the richly textured and complex history of architecture, landscape architecture, and urban planning and design at Harvard, we hope to establish a means by which to clearly understand our institutional present. Indeed, before considering the impact the GSD has had or might have on design education, we must turn this critique inward and actively engage our own history.

Our interest in this history was provoked by a recent exhibition of GSD archival materials gathered from the Special Collections of the Frances Loeb Design Library. The exhibition included archival photos of young men wearing bow ties, huddled over colored-pencil renderings in a studio with plaster casts of classical capital details mounted on the walls. The objects and photographs seemed as far removed as one could get from the GSD of today. Upon closer inspection, however, these very same images suggest the School's "visual ideology" has not changed significantly in the past 40 years. The duality of these images (both strange and familiar) raised many questions as to what the School signifies. In a surreal way, the archive anticipates the GSD's present. Fragments of current pedagogy, ideology, and departmental interests already exist in the collection. Based on this somewhat disparate continuity, we would like to propose through this compilation that the GSD—rather than being understood merely as a generic assembly of architecture, landscape architecture, and urban planning and design—represents a distinct "visual school of thought."

Even before German architectural critic Heinrich Klotz popularized the myth that Walter Gropius sold the contents of the design library in the late 1930s, the GSD has endured the reputation of being opposed to history. In a curious way the School's repository sustains this myth. Upon visiting our archives, one is immediately faced with huge chronological voids. Decades of work are not represented—as if entire departments were silent for years. It might be interesting to assume that these lapses represent (American) modernism's propensity to purge historicist inclinations, but this preoccupation would bring too much historical significance to bear on what is, in reality, a modest institutional collection. More than likely, the missing components of our history could be written off to haste, non-standard procedure, and, until recently, the lack of a proper repository. Such administrative miscues are far less compelling than the drama of Gropius selling off the precious contents of the library. Nevertheless, the present condition of the archive reveals a correlation between the School's historical consciousness and its ideology—when the ideology of the School was most clear (i.e., under Gropius) there was no need for history.

For our purposes, of course, these large gaps make it extremely difficult to establish a "tight" method of historical inquiry. What we have attempted to do, instead, is forego a thorough or consistent reading of the institution in favor of a more fluid retrospective. As a method of selecting work from the archive, the editors have tried to isolate recurrent themes, projects, and preoccupations alongside anomalies. We have chosen to publish student projects from Core and Option studios, design theses, treatises, which classes students took, how they lived, and what their concerns were while here at Harvard. In effect, we have published a sample catalogue of our archive alongside the student projects of the past year to illustrate how far we have come, what we have chosen to leave behind, and what remains amazingly consistent. In essence, the GSD's collection impressively accentuates the fine line that must exist between consistent pedagogy and institutional lethargy.

Regardless of the School's necessary omissions in the making and maintenance of its archives, it clearly has a deep commitment to the development of students as independent thinkers—even to the extent of surrendering institutional interests for the sake of artistic sovereignty. This feature of knowing when to step aside is perhaps the most distinguished trait of the School and is clearly demonstrated throughout its curriculum and visual history.

Studio Works 6, unlike its predecessors, represents not only a singular moment in time, but also a layered history against which we are able to register the lineage of recent studio work presented in this publication. Perhaps by examining where we are now—alongside where we have come from—we may indeed be able to better understand the good, the bad, the obscure, the embarrassing, and the inspiring things that continue to happen here.

The Editors

THE FIRST YEAR DESIGN CURRICULA

The professional field of architects, landscape architects, and city planners is the shaping of our physical environment for human use.

The objective of the design curriculum for the First Year is twofold:

1. To make the student aware of the nature of the human environment and the forces that form it.

2. To start building the knowledge and skills required to shape that environment as a planner and a designer.

The course in Environmental Design, which is pursued by students from all three professional fields, studies problems of the human habitat in its larger context and culminates in plans for a specific development area. The course in Architectural Design, which is follwed by students of architecture and landscape architecture, continues the studies begun in the Envrironmental Design course, concentrating on study in greater detail of smaller elements of the environment: the dwelling unit itself and its immediate environment.

Both courses are intended to make the student see man, with his needs and technical resources, as the measure of the environment which he creates for himself. Studies will be made to establish criteria based on man's needs and potentialities. These will be alternated with specific case studies in which the criteria established will form the basis for judgment and design.

The design courses are complemented by the course in Visualization and Graphics, in which the exercises draw upon the design courses for subject matter, thus linking both efforts into a continuous sequence of design and communication.

TEACHING METHODS:

The course will be conducted by means of periodic group discussions, field trips and studio work under criticism. At the completion of various phases of work reviews will be held. Juries, in which other members of the faculty participate, will be held four times during the year. Students are invited to take part in the review and jury discussions.

The work of the course will consist of a series of diverse tasks or problems: some will be investigative, others will be theoretical explorations of design principles, and still others will be design projects for specific situations. These latter projects, which occupy the majority

Architecture 2b, Wood Frame
House. September 1950.
Garber, J.; Carroll, M. E.;
Chapman, R. H.; Eaches, D.
(13.6.B G16m)

Architecture 2b, Wood Frame
House. September 1950.
Takayanagi, T. (13.6.D T14)

LINE
SPACE
VALUE
SOLID
TEXTURE
COLOR
ALPHABET

DESIGN

TITLE PAGE

LINE

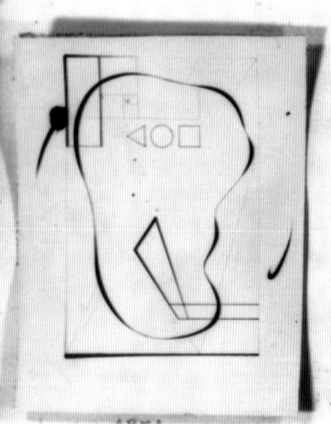

+ AREA

+ SPACE

Designs from the seven visual elements

— VALUE

HU. Sch of Design

Housing Problem

(Problem V for the 2^c classes and the 2^d class)

Problem issued: April 7 at 2 p.m.
Problem due: May 22 at 10 p.m.
Jury: May 23 (Friday)

I. Introduction:

The wholesale bombing and destruction of cities and city-districts during the current world war in Europe has brought forth the problem of replanning and rebuilding cities on the basis of new town-planning and building principles derived mainly from new principles of defense against the destructive effect of war-machines. This far-reaching replanning work is not restricted to single districts and whole cities but includes regional and national planning problems as well. Thus it offers a great opportunity and can even be considered as a challenge for all architects, site planners and town planners to find out the best shape of human settlement to fit the modern warfare of our power-age.

Far-sighted town planners and architects, however, did not need the horrible experience of modern warfare to get ideas "from the wrong reason" for the revision of our present building principles. They got incentive enough from facts surrounding our "peaceful life" and knew that almost all our present planning and building principles grew obsolete long ago because they did not fit the most simple and primary requirements of our power-age. All our cities and settlements are machine-sick! They are machine-sick because they are not designed and built for the

Housing - Study and teach

an expert committee of the American Public Health Association. (Second edition, May 1939, price, 25 cents). Further data will be given on special demand during the hours of criticisms and in the form of special lectures.

VI. Time table for the work on the problem:

It may be assumed that the work on our given problem be a part of a post-war project of the Federal Government and that we - that is our School of Design - stand in competition with other schools of the country for submitting sketchy proposals for a modern organized neighborhood quarter in a new town. For this reason we ought to concentrate all our strength and ability on a good solution of the problem and on good presentation of the plans and models. Since all architectural work in practice is bound to be delivered at prefixed dates, and since organizing and timing one's design work contributes so much to the final success we are induced to try out this method in our present problem and shall criticize and mark it on the dates fixed below:

April 7:	Problem issued.
April 8 to April 15:	Study of the location and working out the first sketches for the general town plan.
April 16:	Class criticism and marking.
April 17 to April 22:	Working out the first sketch of a neighborhood plan.
April 23:	Class criticism and marking.
April 24 to May 1:	Working out the first sketch for a house plan.
May 2:	Class criticism and marking.
May 3 to May 10:	Adjusting the house plan and the neighborhood plan and computing the economic rent of the house type.
May 12:	Class criticism and marking.
May 13 to May 17:	Working out of a model for the neighborhood plan in panel work and for the house plan individually.

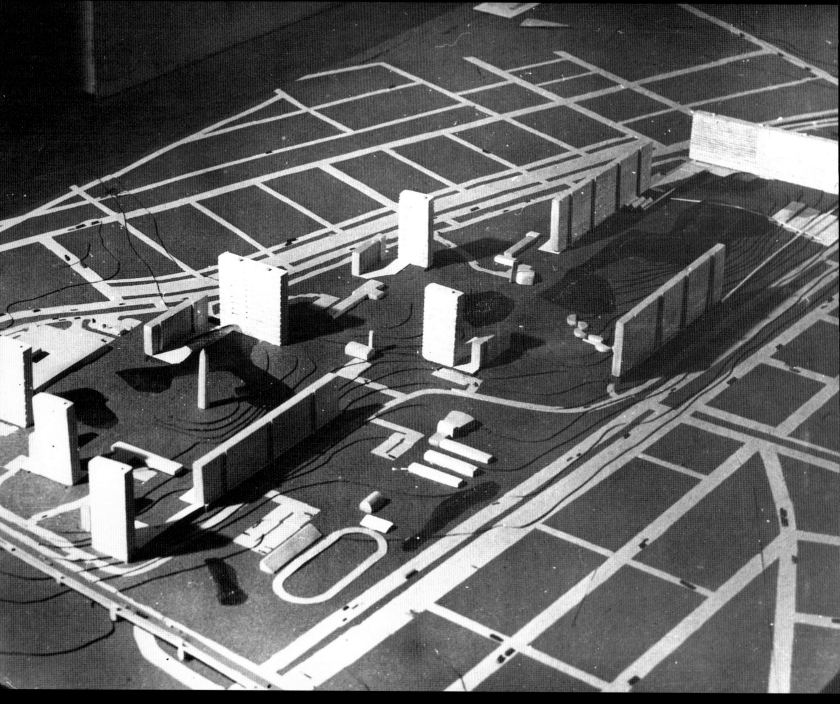

U.D. 2-5ab, Urban Design Studio   **Problem Three**
Monday, Thursday, and Friday at 2:00 p.m.   **Issued: February 5, 1962**
Dean Sert, Professor Tyrwhitt, Mr. Vigier,   **Date Due: March 25, 1962**
with participation of Professor Eliot and
other Faculty   **DESIGNING INTER CITY GROWTH**
Members

1. Purposes

A constantly increasing world population and increasing possibilities of
mobility have led to a proliferation of dwellings miles distant from cities
in all parts of the world. There is no evidence that this trend is decreasing,
and while there are plenty of protests against "urban sprawl," none of the
attempts to control it seem successful. Moreover, the two most influential
forces, highway programs and suburban developers, seem to be motivated
solely by cheapest alignments and quick returns, heedless of the great destruction caused to long term natural assets and the general chaos of inter
city areas.

During this problem period we intend to explore the possibilities of tighter
patterns of design which can harness these forces in such a way that the
anticipated growth of population can take place without strangling or destroying good urban settlements or unspoiled natural features. In particular we are concerned that both the built-up areas and the open land acquire
shapes that can be sensed, and a compactness and efficiency of design.

Each student is expected to develop in some detail a schematic solution which
handles a specific set of criteria. These individually-determined criteria
will be evaluated by the instructors with the intention that the class as a
whole should work on as wide a range of alternatives as possible.

The design of inter city growth will also form the basis of a day of panel
discussions with invited guests at the Urban Design Conference, April 13
and 14. Members of the Urban Design Studio will be included in three
panels, which will discuss three major types of channelling inter city growth:
constellations of towns, inter city corridors and concentrated peripheral
growth (referred to for simplicity as dots, lines, and rings).

2. Organization

Work will be divided into three stages: Historical Background (2 weeks),
Personal Criteria (1 week), Personal Solutions (4 weeks).

NOTES

LANDSCAPE DESIGN
I
HALF YEAR ~ 1900

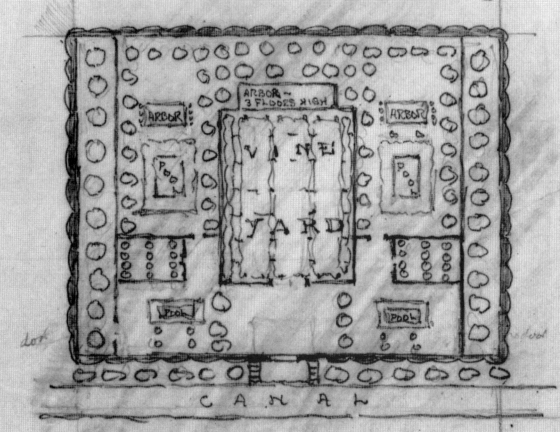

EGYPTIAN GARDEN
from a wall painting

CANAL

Partitions are wall in every case
Note that 3 story arbor overlooked
the whole formally

NB for an account of the plants grown
in the old Egyptian Gardens
see a book by Franz Woenig
called " Die Pflanzen im Alten Aegypten "

from:
Monumenti dell' Egitto
E Della Nubia by
IPPOLTO ROSELLINI
PISA ~ MDCCCXXXIV

AS
Harvard Library
Oct 5 - 1900

L, A.

Thursday, March
Mr. Watson will meet
for a talk on Vegetab
in the afternoon, 1.3
the plans drawn up

I. A.

3, 1916. 10.-11. a.m.,
he members of L.A. 8
e gardens, and
- 3.30, will criticize
oday, March 16, 1916.

CORE STUDIOS

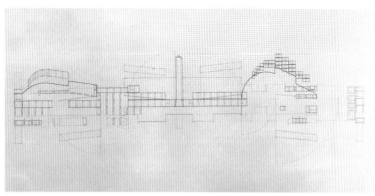

Steven Hsun Lee MArch '01, Analysis Drawing of Carpenter Center

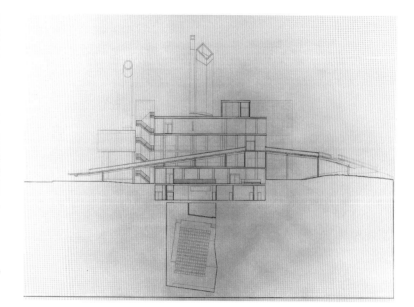

Introduction to Design and Visual Studies in Architecture

Rocco Ceo

Ned Collier

Darell Fields, *coordinator*

George Liaropoulos-Legendre

Tim Love

Monica Ponce de Leon

During the first semester, projects concentrated on the complex relationship between built and drawn representations of architecture. The first project, "survey and analysis," required students to capture, comprehend, and dissect the supposed reality of existing buildings within the "flat space" of orthographic drawings. This proximity between the building and its representation intensifies the technical and conceptual problems that emerge when distinct manifestations of architecture are intended to approximate one another. The requirement to create a likeness between three-dimensional space and its two-dimensional representation encouraged intense observation and exacting formal definitions.

The second project asked the students to reverse the process of the first by interpreting a set of drawings of an existing building as a three-dimensional context for the intervention of an elevator. The building's dynamic section was so tightly calibrated with alternating centralized and bifurcated plans that the intervention of the continuous vertical passage, no matter how well integrated on any given level, would inevitably interrupt a room, stair, or passage on another level. The problem was to absorb the elevator into the rigorous formal coherence of the given building. In the second stage of the project, the building was assumed to be re-situated ninety degrees with respect to its street address. The problem—to readjust the plan, section, and elevations of the building to address a different "front"—required a sustained negotiation between existing and proposed compositional strategies discovered during the initial elevator intervention.

The last project, a recreation center, introduced the idea of "program" as a formal determinant. In this case, squash, bowling, and batting became the progenitors of both fixed spatial arrangements and residual spaces. The challenge was to design a building that synthesized the inherently determined sizes, proportions, tendencies of orientation, materials, fenestration (or lack thereof), structural spans and other internal pressures within the limiting boundaries of an urban site. During the development of the project, critical focus was given to the configurative logic of the programmatic constituents. This spatial composition was then recalibrated to acquire urban specificity and symbolic resonance.

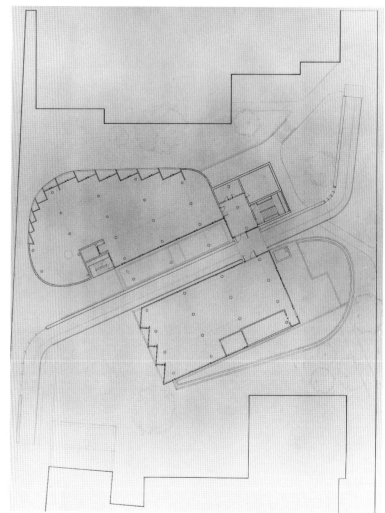

Yehre Suh MArch '01, Cross Section and Plan of Carpenter Center

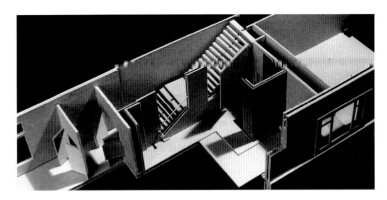

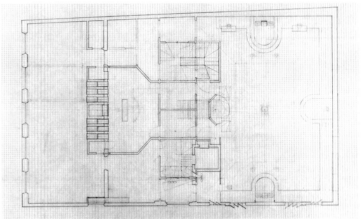

Christina A. Marsh MArch '01, Model View and Plans, Elevator Intervention

Amy Korte MArch '01, Model View and Plan, Elevator Intervention

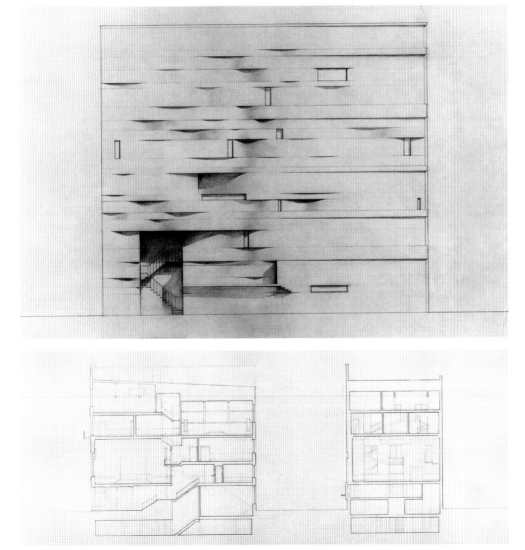

Heather Walls MArch '01, Elevation and Sections, Elevator Intervention

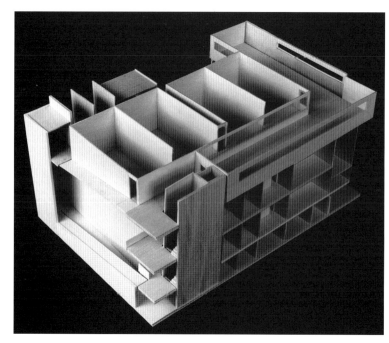

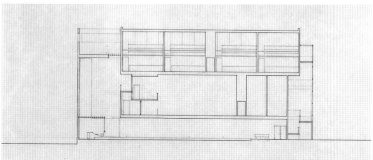

Anne Brockelman MArch '01, Model View and Section, Recreation Center

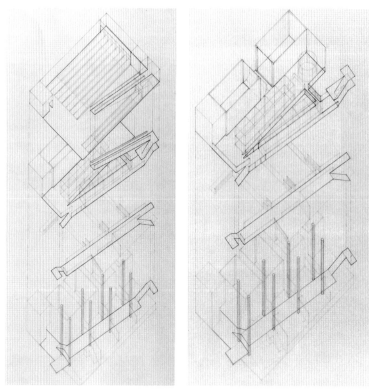

Tinchuck Agnes Ng '01, Axonometric Views, Recreation Center

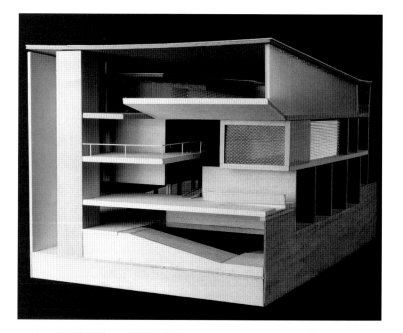

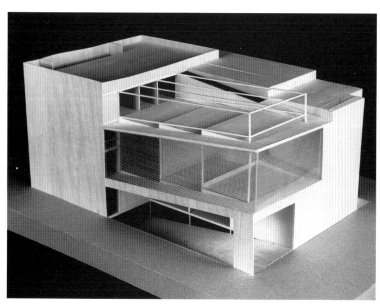

Eric Olsen MArch '01, Model View, Recreation Center

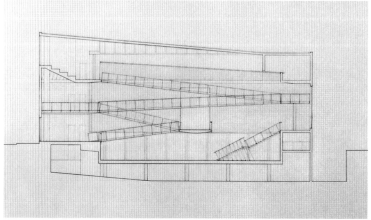

Steven Hsun Lee '01, Model View and Longitudinal Section, Recreation Center

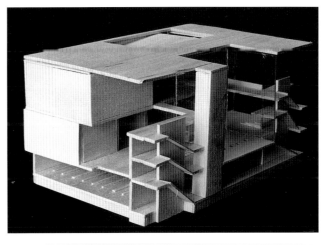

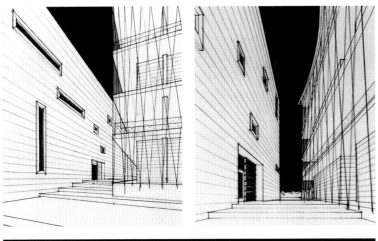

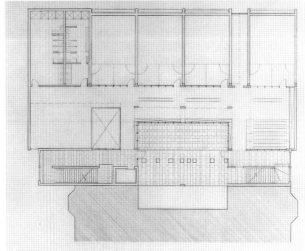

Brian Mulder MArch '01, Model View and Plan, Recreation Center

Kristen Giannattasio MArch '01, Perspective Views and Model View, Recreation Center

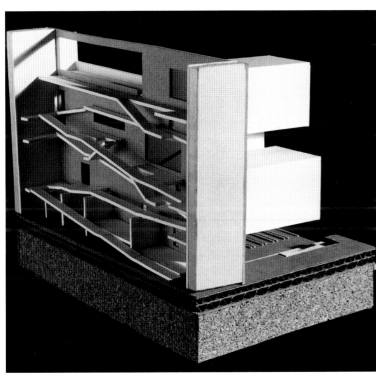

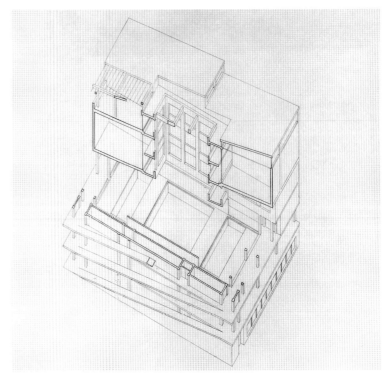

Lucia Allais MArch '01, Model View, Recreation Center

Nicholas Maynard MArch '01, Section/Axonometric, Recreation Center

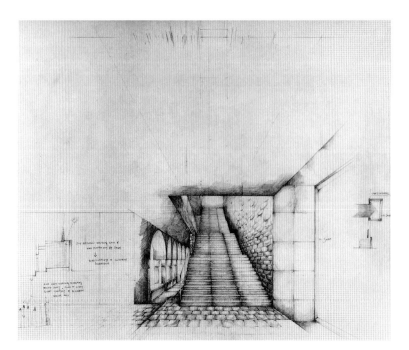

David Goodman MArch '01, Projective Working Drawing, Isabella Stewart Gardner Museum

Introduction to Design and Visual Studies in Architecture

Alex Anmahian

Scott Cohen, *coordinator*

Tim Love

Monica Ponce de Leon

Luis Rojo de Castro

T. Kelly Wilson

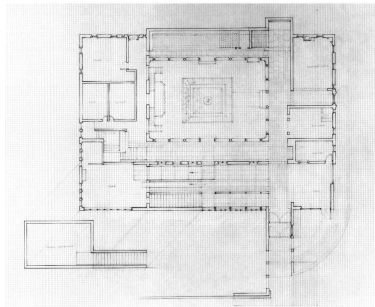

Dana S. Cho MArch '01, Entry Condition and Plan, Isabella Stewart Gardner Museum

This semester involved beginning to reflect upon the architect's responsibility and privilege as identity-maker, on the one hand, and on the architect's role as choreographer and coordinator of disparate forces, on the other. The projects served as vehicles through which to elaborate and articulate disciplinary conventions through formal invention.

Two projects required making architectural proposals legible and intricate enough to be traced back to multiple formal and aesthetic impulses. Though clearly limited in scope, each circumstance posed a predicament of identity, difficult to resolve, within a hypothetically familiar social and physical context.

The first project asked for a new entrance and decompressed interior sequence for the Isabella Stewart Gardner Museum—the current identity of which lies ambiguously on the spectrum between institutional building and outside-in palazzo. The second project, a new building to consolidate the Anthropology Department at Harvard, produced consequences for the already compromised identities of entrance sequences to surrounding buildings and campus yards.

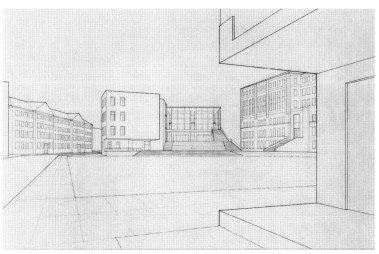

Mario D'Artista MArch '01, Perspective View, Anthropology Department

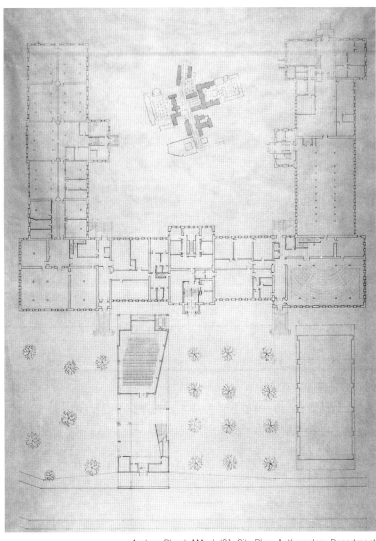

Andrew Plumb MArch '01, Site Plan, Anthropology Department

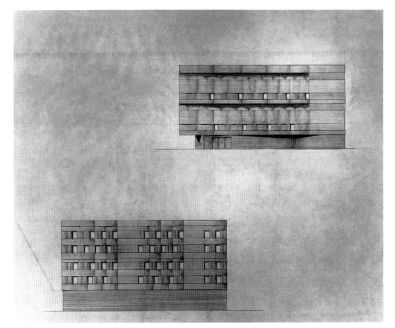

Andrew Varela MArch '01, Elevation Studies, Anthropology Department

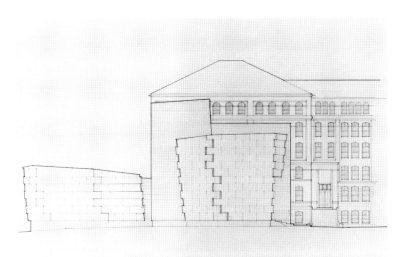

Kristen Giannattasio MArch '01, Elevation, Anthropology Department

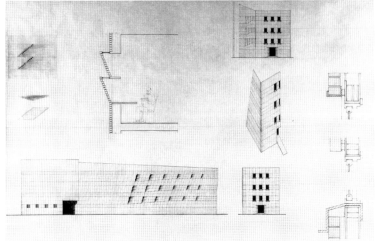

Tinchuck Agnes Ng MArch '01, Study Model and Elevation Studies, Anthropology Department

Jenny Elkus MArch '01, Section, Anthropology Department

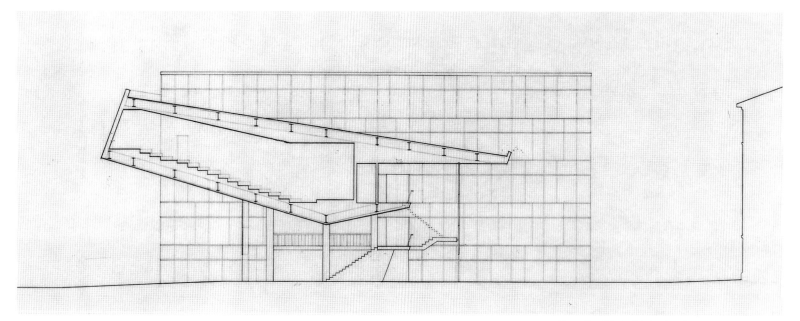

Mona Ying MArch '01, Section, Anthropology Department

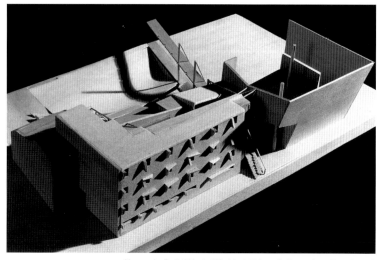

Young-Ju Baik MArch '01, Model View, Anthropology Department

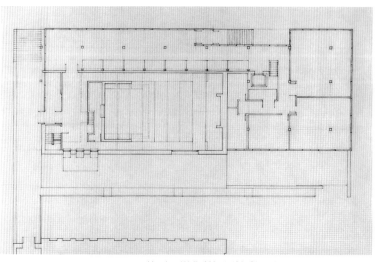

Heather Walls MArch '01, Plan, Anthropology Department

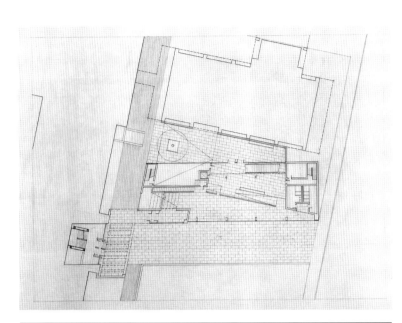

Cynthia Lordan MArch '01, Model View, Anthropology Department

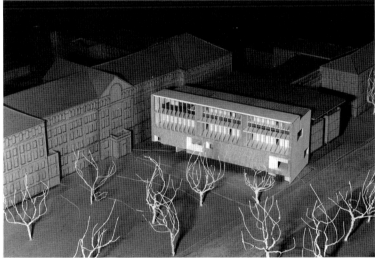

Steven Hsun Lee MArch '01, Plan and Model View, Anthropology Department

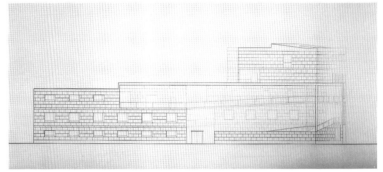

Sebastian Guivernau MArch '01, Elevation, Anthropology Department

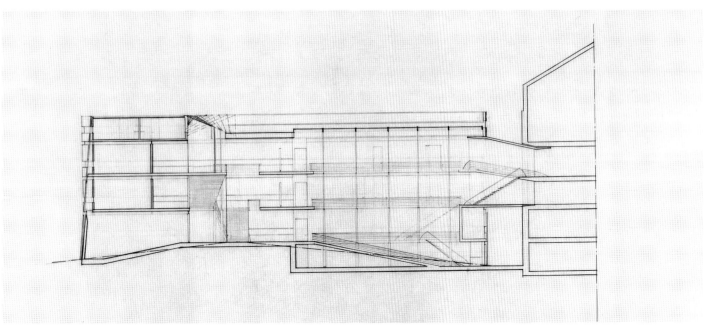

Kristine Synnes MArch '01, Section, Anthropology Department

Masatoyo Ogasawara MArch '00, Model View and Concept Model of Material

Library and Media Tech in South End, Boston:
Architectonics of Internal and External

Jude LeBlanc

Jonathan Levi

Daniel Monk

Toshiko Mori, *coordinator*

Mark Mulligan

James Williamson

The library is an ancient and historical type of building that still holds its place in our society as a place of reading, research, and gathering. The transformation from its original role as an archive of documents set aside exclusively for scholarly or ecclesiastical purposes, to the circulating library for general public use, reflects changes in societal attitudes regarding the relationship between modes of disseminating information and a more generalizing conception of humanity.

The library is a building type where the site strategy, program, materiality, and tectonics of the building can reflect the philosophy of the architect in a particularly potent way. It is ideally suited to put forth a cohesive argument for an architect's intentions regarding both its geographical place in the city, and its temporal place in history. An argument is formed by each student with reference to the polemic of printing versus digital media and technology and the polemic it may propose to society at large.

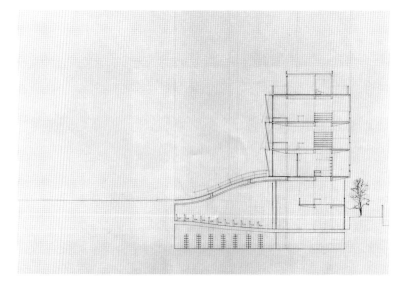

The library, through its tectonic construct, strives to express in a specific architectural language, the balance between its internal and external elements. Human activities such as research, reading, gathering, and their relationship to books, other media, space, and light form the core internal relationship of the library. At the same time, a library assumes an external and urban public presence to announce its role within society.

It was our pedagogical goal to form a cohesive set of documents including drawings, models, and texts that described and expressed the originality and the creativity of the individual student's thesis.

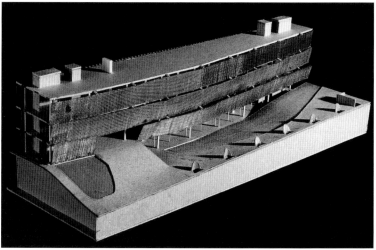

Achyut Kantawala MArch '00, Section and Model View

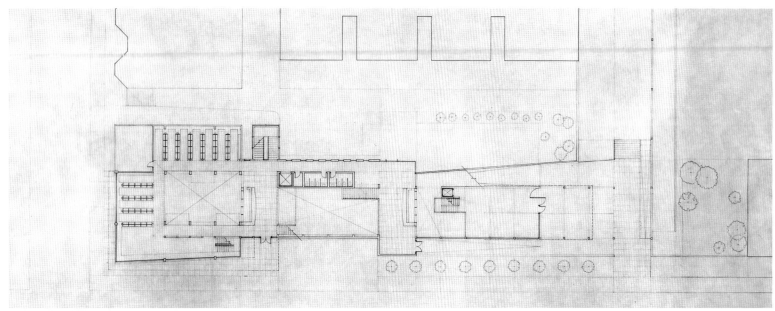

Christine N. Mueller MArch '00, Plan and Model View

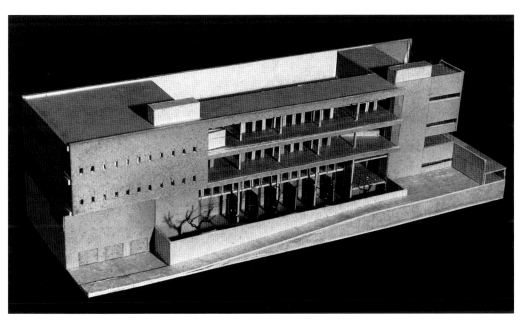

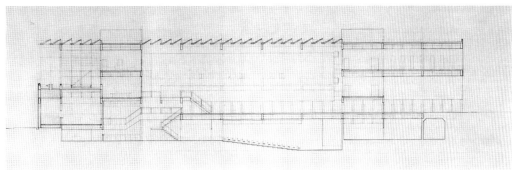

Jennifer Lee MArch '00, Model View and Section

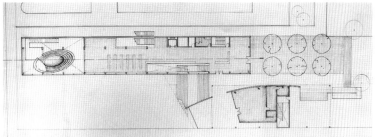

David Y. Chun MArch '00, Model View and Plan

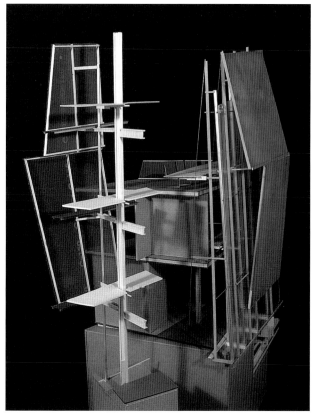

Abel Portal MArch '00, Model View

Chee Keong Lin MArch '00, Perspective Views

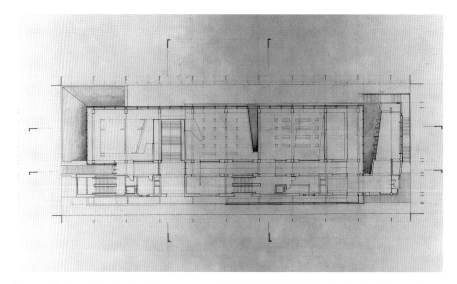

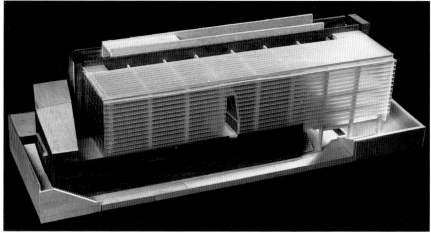

Chanjoong Kim MArch '00, Ground Floor Plan and Model View

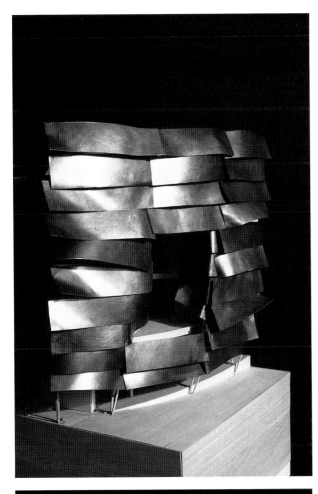

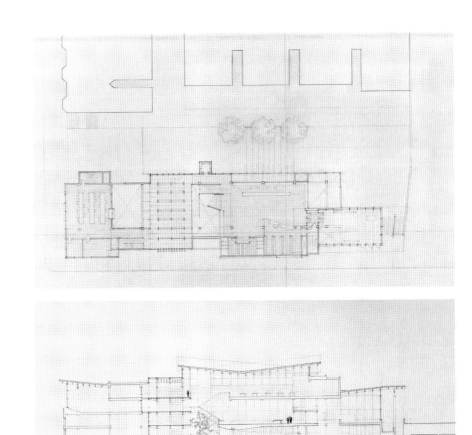

Tom Robinson MArch '00, Plan and Section

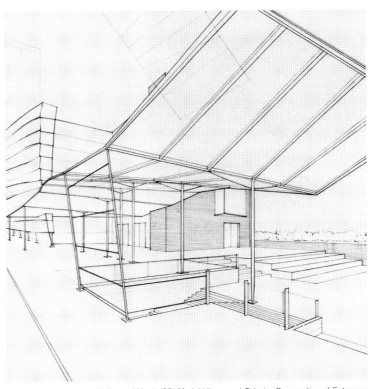

Jill Porter MArch '00, Model Views and Exterior Perspective of Entrance

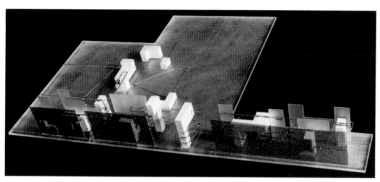

Chee Keong Lin MArch '00, Model View

Design of Housing / Relationships of Scale

Ned Collier

Darell Fields, *coordinator*

Jude LeBlanc

Sandro Marpillero

Mark Mulligan

James Williamson

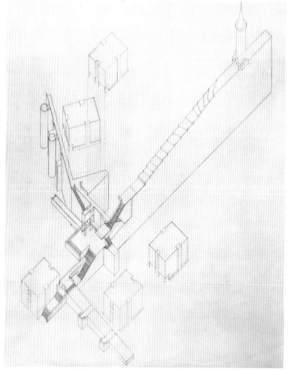

Kuen-Feng Chen MArch '00, Circulation Axonometric

The fourth semester core studio sets up a semester-long research in housing. The notion of scale establishes a thematic study aimed toward understanding how design thinking establishes structural similarities among diverse urban artifacts and how these relate to larger conceptual/physical contexts. In terms of methodology, the curriculum joins analysis and design as necessarily linked and reiterative. Throughout the course of the semester students are required to develop concepts and strategies that will allow them to work simultaneously—through the implementation of housing—on the city and in the city.

This particular adaptation of the studio was structured around three modes of investigation:

The "Analytical" mode was understood as a structured series of interpretations. This entailed the documentation/formulation of social and cultural facts and their relation to spatial and physical representations.

The "Type/Precedent" mode provided personal contact with an excellent (or not so excellent) example of housing. Through documentation and analysis, the essential requirements of a dwelling were studied through the example of a highly developed design.

Finally, the "Programmatic Intervention" mode called for devising a housing program and its design within a proposed site. An architectural argument, based upon the discoveries of the research of the semester, held the project together across scales and determined which elements were to be critically represented.

The sum-total of these investigations produced a critical construct defined as "typomorphology." Typomorphological analysis describes volumetric and spatial urban form (morphology) in terms of classifications of building and open space by type (typology). This technique considers all scales from the small garden room to the urbanized region, characterizes urban form as temporal, and emphasizes the urban parcel (or lot) as a linking element between the building scale and the city scale. The urban analysis structures conceptual and physical matrices for housing and, at the same time, describes multiple and distinct forms of urbanity within the city plan. Typomorphology cultivates the idea that housing, in and of itself, is a complex social fact.

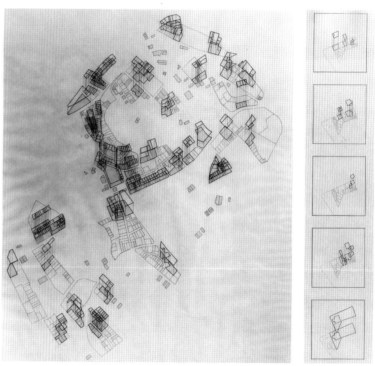

William S. Bryant MArch '00, Three-dimensional Site Study and Morphological Site Studies

Enrique Ramon MArch '00, View Looking South

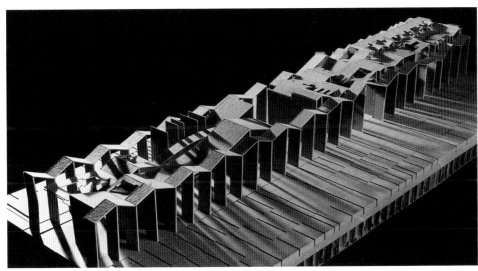

Sung Won Yoon MArch '00, Conceptual Model

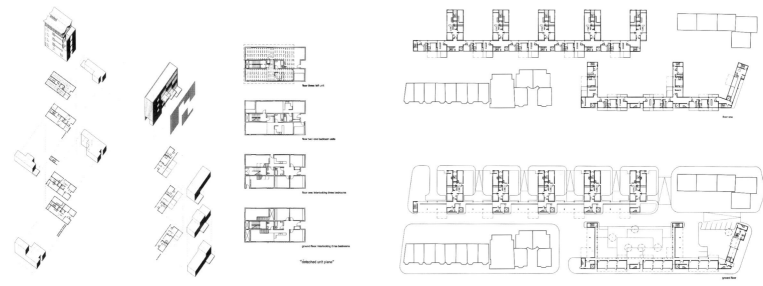

Juan Manuel Villafañe MArch '00, Unit Diagrams and Plans

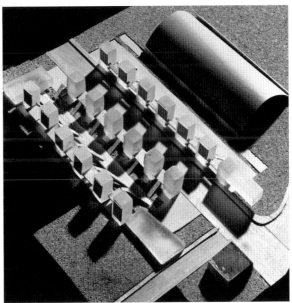

Hunter Tura MArch '00, Analysis Model, Overall Site Strategy Model, and Unit Detail Model

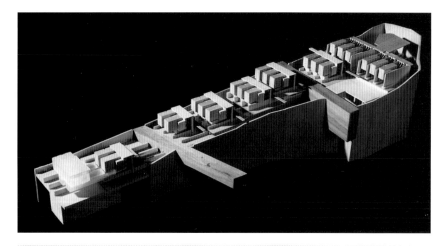

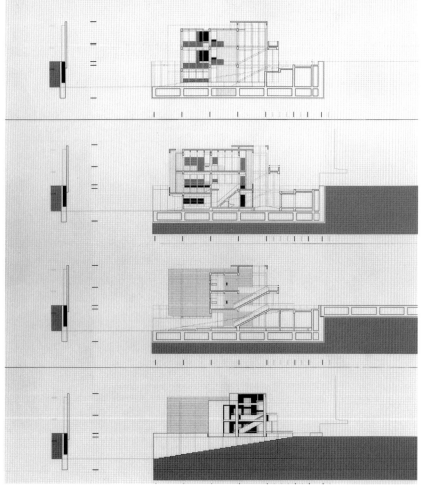

Chanjoong Kim MArch '00, Model View and Sections

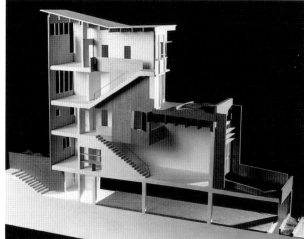

Tom Robinson MArch '00, Model Views

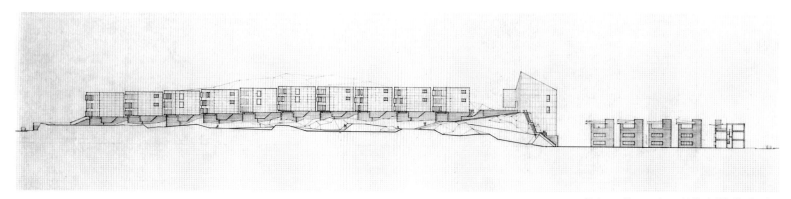

Chatpong Chuenrudeemol MArch '00, Site Section

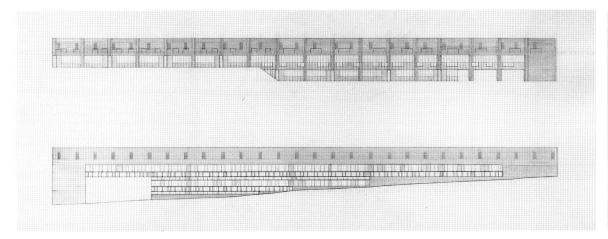

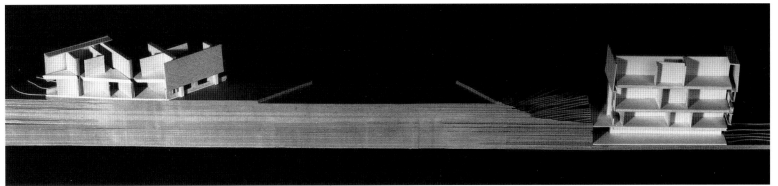

Jeannie Kim MArch '00, Elevations, Site Analysis, and Model View

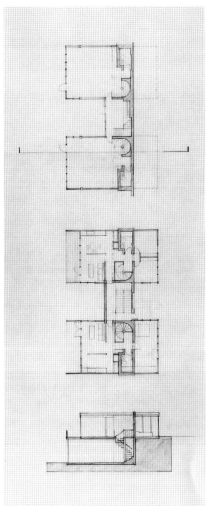
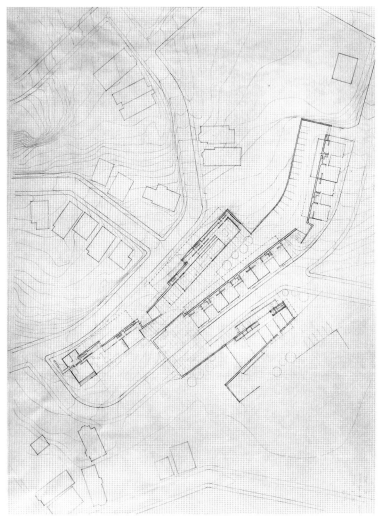

Lynn I. Hsu MArch '00, Unit Plans and Section, and Site Plan

Megan Mann MLA '00, Sections of Clay Landform Models

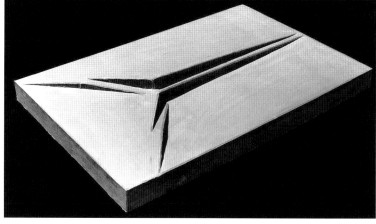

Jacob E. Petersen MLA '00, Model View

Landscape Architecture Design

Anita Berrizbeitia, *coordinator*

Mark Klopfer

George Hargreaves and Kirt Rieder, *workshop*

The first of four core studios, this course introduced landscape as a field focused on the intersection of general design principles and theories with the specifics of a site and its cultural and environmental context. The studio began with analytical and interpretive studies of a built landscape. This project exposed complexity and multivalency in landscape, and it served to undo certain preconceptions so that the student could acquire tools for conceptualization.

Subsequently, a series of short intensive workshops focused on considerations of the ground plane and the section. Here students investigated typologies of natural and constructed landforms and their potential for expression, as well as relations among the body, movement, horizon, and scale. The final studio problem was focused on the generative roles of program and site. By confronting a program of ambitious dimensions in a resistant site context, the project examined issues of complex and overlapping site geometries, landscape thresholds, and the intersection of multiple social realms.

The studio was taught in conjunction with an allied course in representation, which afforded the student a way of engaging essential drawing conventions as tools for visualization and examination. Units of study in technology and plants in design were also integrated with the studio problems to give emphasis to the studio as a site of learning and synthesis throughout the curriculum.

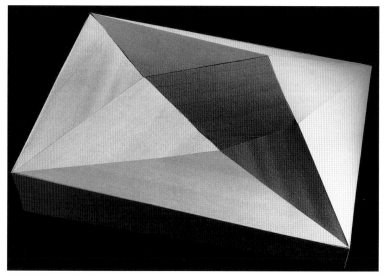

Harold Koda MLA '00, Model View

Megan Mann MLA '00, Model View, Cambridge Rindge and Latin School

Jacob E. Petersen MLA '00, Model View, Cambridge Rindge and Latin School

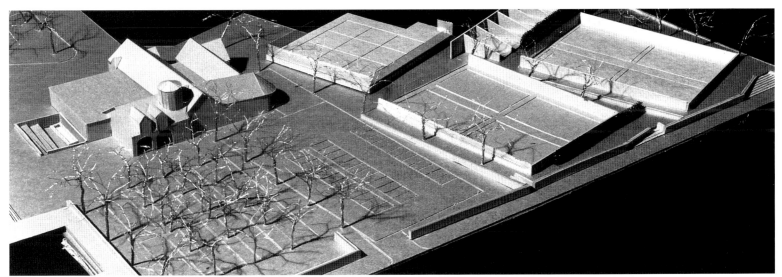

Harold Koda MLA '00, Model View, Cambridge Rindge and Latin School

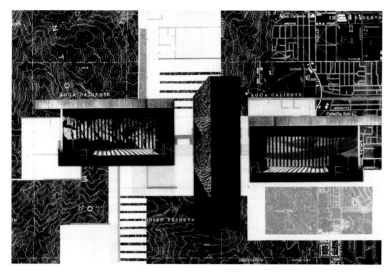

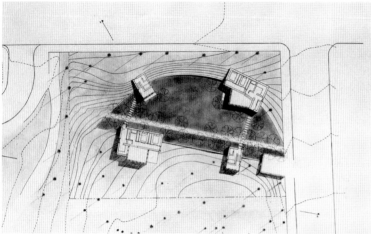

Ruth Webb MLA '00, Precedent Analysis and Plan

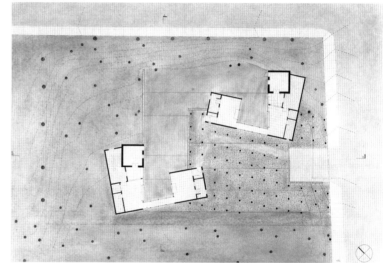

Landscape Architecture Design

Gary Hilderbrand, *coordinator*
Holly Getch Clarke
Mark Klopfer

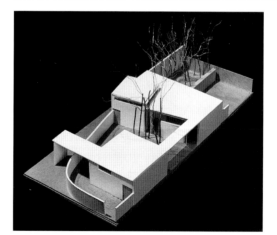

The second of four core studios in Landscape Architecture, this course pursues forms and processes of the garden in its most essential manifestation—domestic space. The semester began with an investigation of the modern detached house and the ideologies that inform its language, its building technology, and its relation to site. The second exercise required the student to engage a set of prescribed formal issues in the design of a house and garden without a site, seeking a reciprocity of formal and spatial motivations inside and out. In the next problem, this non-site proposition was transported to a narrow infill lot, and the student proceeded to incrementally adjust and transform the hypothesis according to issues of a real site and context. The final problem involved a more strongly foregrounded landscape and yet another formal and material transformation, the doubling of the house—where the issues of shared space raised another dimension of garden-making.

The repetitive nature of these studio problems forced the student to hold on to a limited set of ideas and figures that could be transformed through new circumstances. In this way, the topographical, ecological, and tectonic factors of site were consistently weighed against the essential formal logic of the project, and the primacy of formal ideas over circumstantial realities was challenged.

Andrew J. Gutterman MLA '00, View Through
Entrance Grove, Plan, Model View, and Plan Study

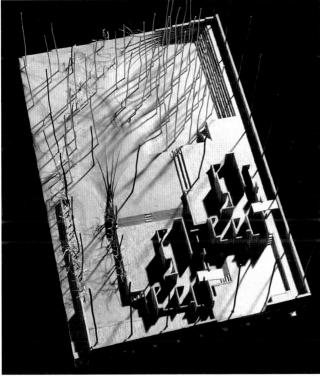

Jacob E. Petersen MLA '00, Perspective View and Model Views

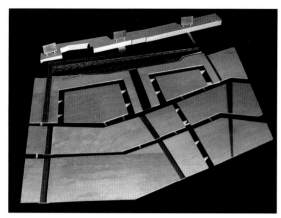

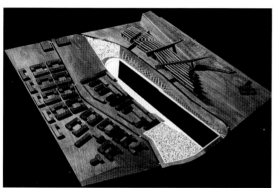

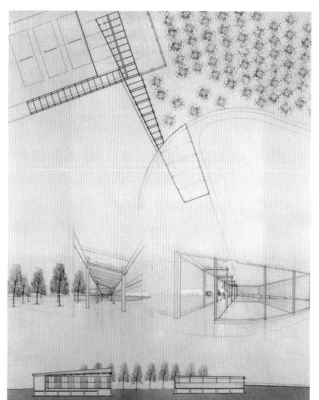

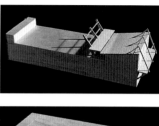

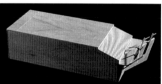

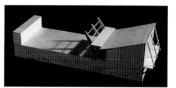

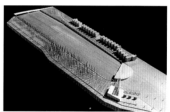

Karen M. M'Closkey MLA '99, Model Views, Plan, Perspectives, and Section

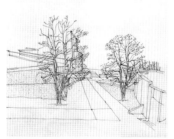

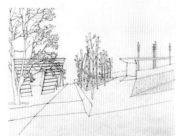

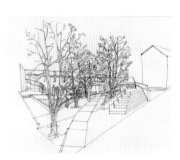

Planning of Design of Landscapes

Elizabeth Dean Hermann
George Hargreaves, *coordinator*
Leonard Newcomb
Rossana Vaccarino

The third of four core studios in Landscape Architecture, this course pursued the role of landscape systems—topographic conditions, hydrologic characteristics, habitat, transportation networks, and social structures—in the reconfiguration of urban communities. Focused on the neighborhoods and waterfront edges of Charlestown, Massachusetts, students investigated limited design strategies that could instigate the recapture of neglected or disused sites. Building on the skills and intellectual constructs framed in previous core studios, students were expected to move beyond the conceptual argument of the project toward the engagement of implementation strategies and tectonic detail.

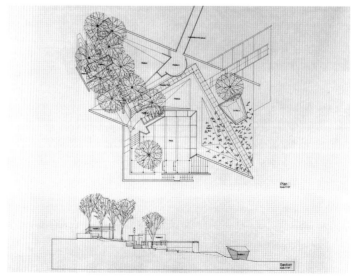

Carlos A. Torres MLA '99, Perspective Views, Plan, and Section

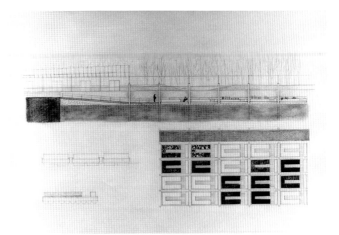

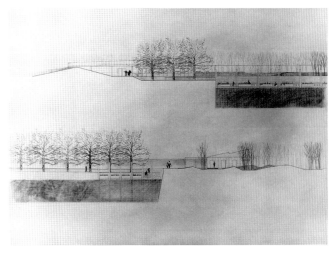

Kristen Cardoza First MLA '99, Model View of Little Mystic Channel,
Section/Elevation and Detail Plan, and Section/Elevations

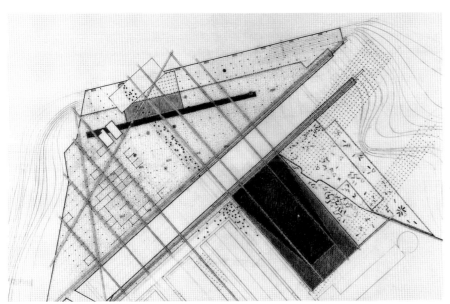

Nathaniel S. Cormier MLA '99, Preliminary Plan for Intervention

Letitia Tormay MLA '99, Model View

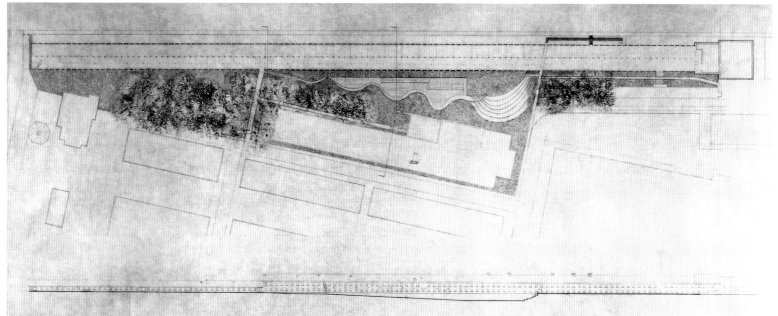

Stephen Young MLA '99, Model View, Plan, and Section

Sara Peschel MLA '99, Model View "Cathedral Under the Tobin," and Model View

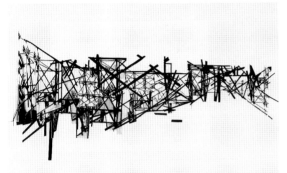

Nicholas Tobier MLA '00, Plan, Section, and Elevation; Obstructions and Apertures; Perspective of Path; and Model View

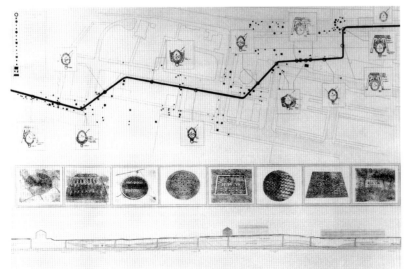

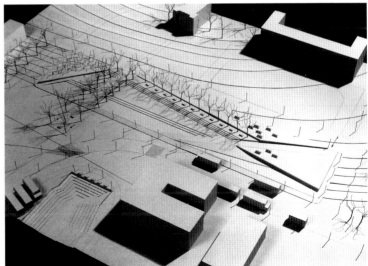

Allyson Mendenhall MLA '99, Map of Manhole Covers and Sewers and Model View

Planning and Design of Landscapes

Anita Berrizbeitia
Joseph Disponzio
Robert France
Carl Steinitz, *coordinator*

This core studio explored landscape planning and design, ranging from community-site location to the detailed design of special places. It focused on the design of a new community for members of a religion (specified by the team), to be located in an expanding, historic New England town, Petersham, Massachusetts.

Working at diverse scales, three-person teams prepared a multiple land-use site plan. Individual students designed key elements within the overall project.

The major objectives were to locate and design a large and complex landscape development and to develop abilities in organization, teamwork, and complex design decision-making of sometimes conflicting objectives with particular emphasis on the relationship between social needs and landscape design at several scales.

Cynthia Jensen MLA '99, Nancy L. Parmentier MLA '99, and Carolyn Pendelton-Parker MLA '99, Model Views of "Ten Thousand of One Taoist Community"

Kristen Cardoza First MLA '99, Karen M. M'Closkey MLA '99, and Allyson Mendenhall MLA '99, Model Views of "New Amish Community"

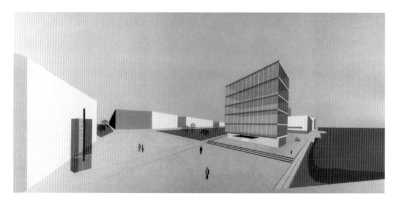

Elements of Urban Planning and Design

Lee Cott
Douglas Dolezal
John Driscoll
Kathryn Firth
Alex Krieger, *coordinator*
François Vigier

This studio is one of two foundation courses for the Urban Design and Urban Planning degree programs. It emphasizes the development of a critical awareness of how the physical city affects and is affected by social, cultural, and economic factors. Conducted as both a studio and seminar/workshop, design problems tackle issues such as: 1) the interpretation of both traditional and contemporary paradigms for urban and suburban design; 2) how urban concepts are represented; 3) the interrelationships among streets, blocks, districts, parks, transportation corridors, and other components that make up contemporary urban environments; 4) singular urban ideologies and their relationship to the history of urban design; 5) as well as the implications of specific design strategies on the formulation of public policy.

Five related exercises introduced students to the basic elements of urban planning and design. The first design problem, an investigation of alternative configurations for Boston's City Hall Plaza and the surrounding area called Government Center, involved a consideration of essential characteristics of urban place-making.

The second exercise dealt with interventions and extensions to the city fabric by investigating the impact of a common historical catalyst for major urban change. Using nineteenth-century maps of European cities as a starting point, students prepared new city plans that responded to the introduction of a new form of transportation—the railroad—and its required network of infrastructure. The third exercise used a similar format to design a highway alignment on mid-century maps of several American cities.

The next exercise focused on housing and place-making in a suburban context. Beginning with an examination of contemporary definitions and perceptions of the suburb, students then tested the suitability and/or adaptability of more conventional urban patterns to a suburban condition by producing designs for a housing precinct based upon the research of a well-known prototype.

Finally, students developed re-use paradigms for urbanized districts whose original uses and purposes have, with modernization, become marginal or obsolete. Students focused on several Boston districts and on emerging long-range planning initiatives to recast their fortunes by promoting them as the backbone for the city's growing economic strength in the bioscience, medical research, and high technology industries. The aim of the exercise was a consideration of the role that urban design can play in the reinterpretation and/or economic resurgence of parts of the city that are presently assumed to be underutilized, undervalued, and in need of "reinvention."

Osamu Sassa MAUD '99, Perspective of Entry Plaza, Site Organization, and Perspective of Atrium, Columbia Point

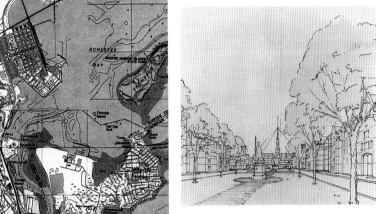

Steven S. Scapicchio MAUD '99, Site Plan, Aerial View, and Perspective Views, Columbia Point

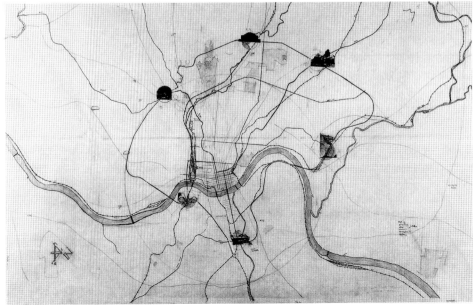

Albert Marichal MAUD '99, Plan of Cincinnati

Heather Culp MUP '99, Mari Morgen KSG, Miro Weinberger KSG, and Wesley Wirth MLA '98, Short Term, Medium Term, and Long Term Plans

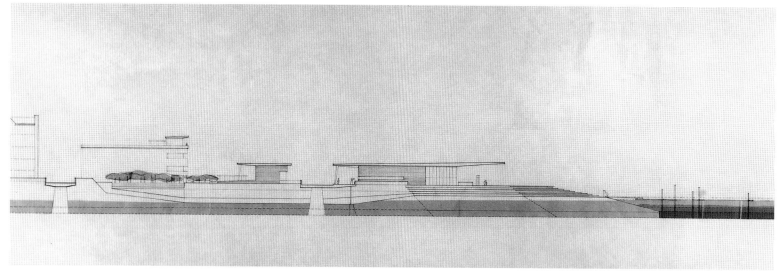

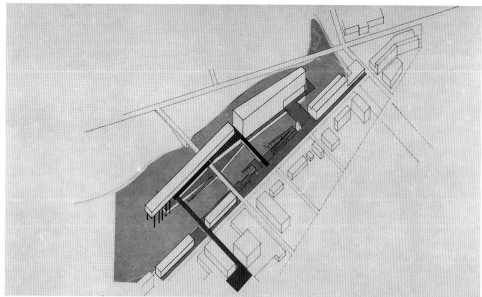

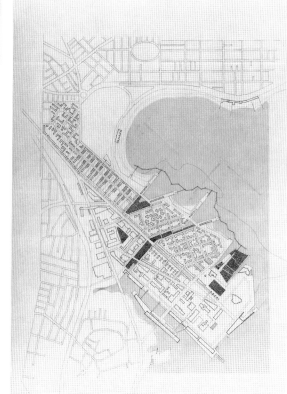

Michelle Cramer MAUD '99, Section, Axonometric View, and Site Plan, Columbia Point

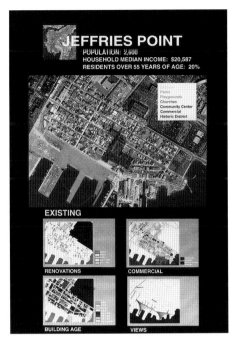

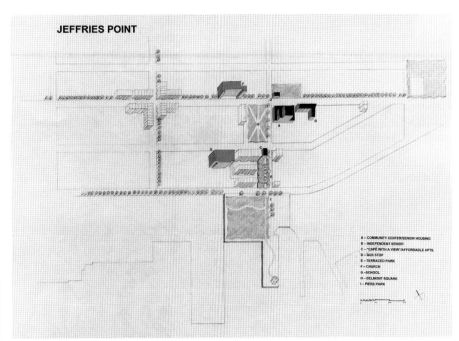

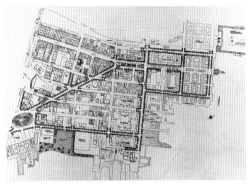

Sara Elliott MUP '99, Erika Oliver MUP '99, David Robbins MLA '98, Judit Szilagyi KSG, Jeffries Point Analysis, Jeffries Point Neighborhood Plan, Perspective View from Maverick Square to Waterfront, Perspective View of Waterfront Walk, and Central Square/Maverick Square Master Plan

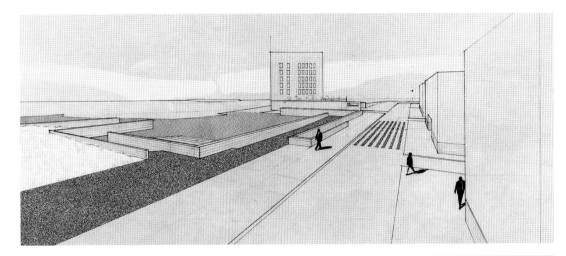

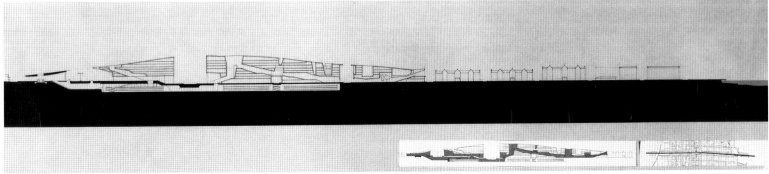

Victor Sant'Anna MAUD '99, Perspective View and Site Section, Columbia Point

Architecture 2d, Faculty
Housing Survey, March
1954. Maki, F. (6.2F M29m2)

Architecture 2d, Faculty
Housing Survey, March
1954. Maki, F. (6.2F M29m1)

Architecture 2d, Faculty
Housing Survey, March
1954. Goodwin, A. P.
(6.2F Go5m1)

Architecture 2b	HARVARD UNIVERSITY — GSD	Issued: April 5, 1948
Currie		Due: ~~May 12~~ May 12, 1948
Harkness		Jury: May 13, 1948
Nagel	PROBLEM IV	

BLOOD TRANSFUSION CENTER FOR SYDNEY, AUSTRALIA

The Australian Red Cross Society, New South Wales Division, proposes the building of a new Blood Donor Center in Sydney. The Society has procured the property indicated on an attached sketch. The land is very expensive, and the Society wishes to use it quite intensively.

The original plan was to demolish the old two story garage covering most of the site, retain the five-story building in the north-east corner of the block, and build a six-story building encompassing the existing five-story building. The new building was to house the general administrative offices of the Red Cross, an auditorium, and various other Red Cross functions. In this building, the Blood Donor Center was to occupy approximately one and one half stories.

As the above scheme would entail a very large, expensive, and time-consuming building operation at a time of stringent material shortages in Australia, it is now suggested that the existing five-story building be retained for the most essential Red Cross administrative functions, that a new and completely separate building be immediately constructed on the westernmost portion of the block to meet the needs of the Blood Donor Service, and that the center of the block be retained for a future tower-type office building to fulfill the larger Red Cross requirements. It is further suggested that the Blood Donor Center be designed with a view to being ultimately linked with the future large office building.

The attached description of the operation of the Blood Donor Center and Outline of Requirements was prepared by Dr. Walsh, of the Australian Red Cross, with the original scheme in mind, namely the incorporation of the Center into a larger Red Cross building.

For the purposes of this problem, Dr. Walsh acts as the client, and will extend and modify his original program in discussion with the class and/or by written addenda.

Drawings and model required:

Plans of all floors, elevations, section or sections at 1/8" = 1'-0".

Model at 1/8" = 1'-0". (Base to include entire block, showing site development and suggested location and massing of future building.)

Sketch perspective of some feature of the design, either interior or exterior.

Typical wall section through roof, window, one typical floor, and footing - at 1½" = 1'-0".

1.924 A

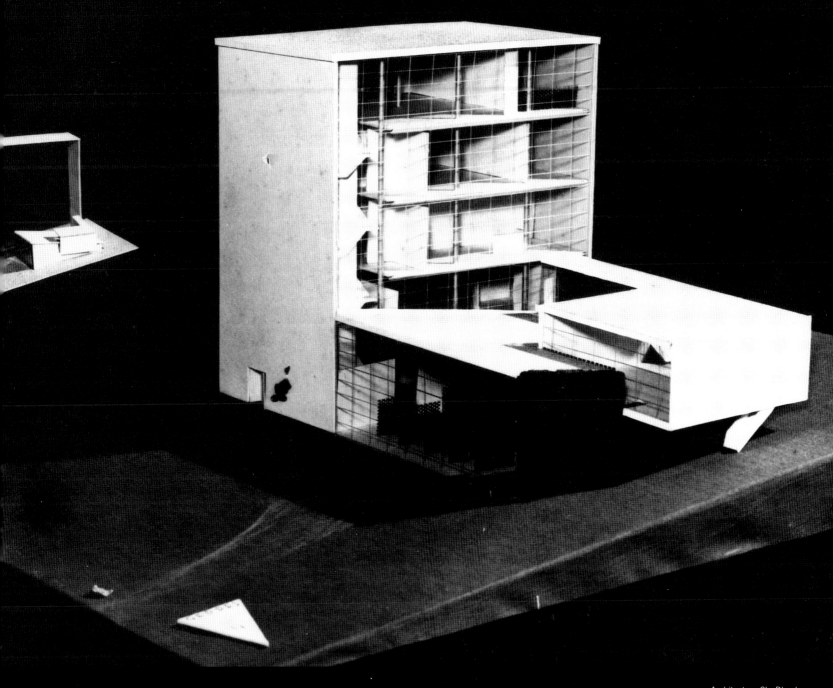

Architecture 2b, Blood
Transfusion Center, May
1948. Geddes, R.
(1.924A G27m)

10

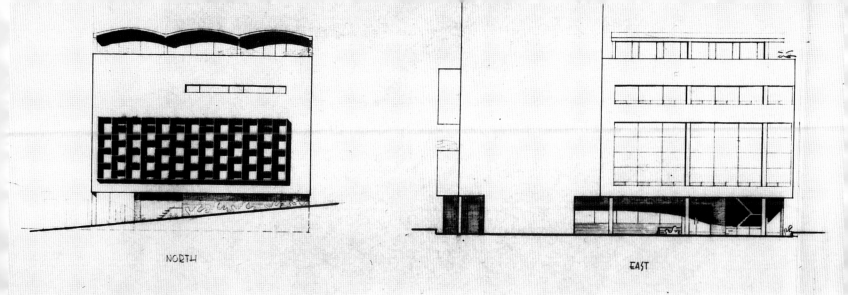

NORTH

EAST

Architecture 2b, Blood
Transfusion Center, May
1948. Brody, S. M.
(1.924A B78 (4)

PERSPECTIVE
OUTGOING WAITING ROOM

Architecture 2–4ab, Church
Studio, May 1955. Haro, J. C.
(3.15a H23)

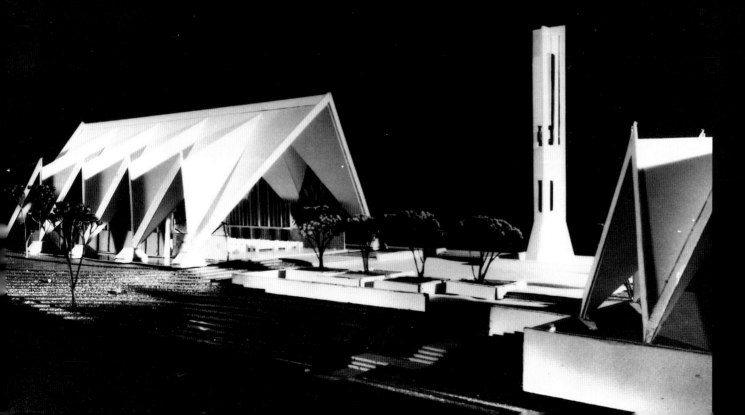

Architecture 2–4ab, Church
Studio, May 1955. Stewart,
J. C. (3.15a St4)

Architecture 2–4ab, Church
Studio, May 1955. Merritt,
H. C. (3.15a M55)

HARVARD UNIVERSITY - GRADUATE SCHOOL OF DESIGN

Arch. 2d   September 25, 1946

Walter Gropius
Leonard Currie   Short Problem

THE DESIGN OF A WEEK-END HOUSE

A young architect with a moderate income has acquired an
attractive house site well away from "the maddening crowd".
He wishes to build a week-end and vacation house for his own
use (with or without family and/or guests), principally in
the summer. As this is not his permanent home, it is his
desire to keep costs and general quality of construction at
a lower level than he would for a year-around house. However,
as the house will advertize his professional services for better or for worse, he wants to achieve a definite architectural
quality in terms of charm and liveability.

Any assumptions may be made as regards the size of family,
geographic location, terrain features, orientation of the site,
availability of materials, etc.

You are the Architect

Requirements:

1. Write a supplementary program describing briefly your assumed situation, location and any special factors which
   may influence your design.

2. Drawings required: Plot plan at 1/32" = 1'-0", floor
   plan or plans at 1/8" = 1'-0", four elevations at
   1/8" = 1'-0", exterior wall section from footing to
   eave or coping at 3/4" = 1'-0".

3. Presentation: Drawings may be executed in any medium
   and on a single sheet of any type and size of paper or
   illustration board.

DUE: Wednesday, October 2, 1946 at 2 p.m.

CRITICISM AND DISCUSSION immediately following submission of
                          drawings.

Image at right: Architecture 2d,
Weekend House, September
1946. McClure, R. A. (6.6C M13)

Outleaf: Architecture 2d,
Weekend House, September
1946. Rudolph, P. M. (6.6C R83)

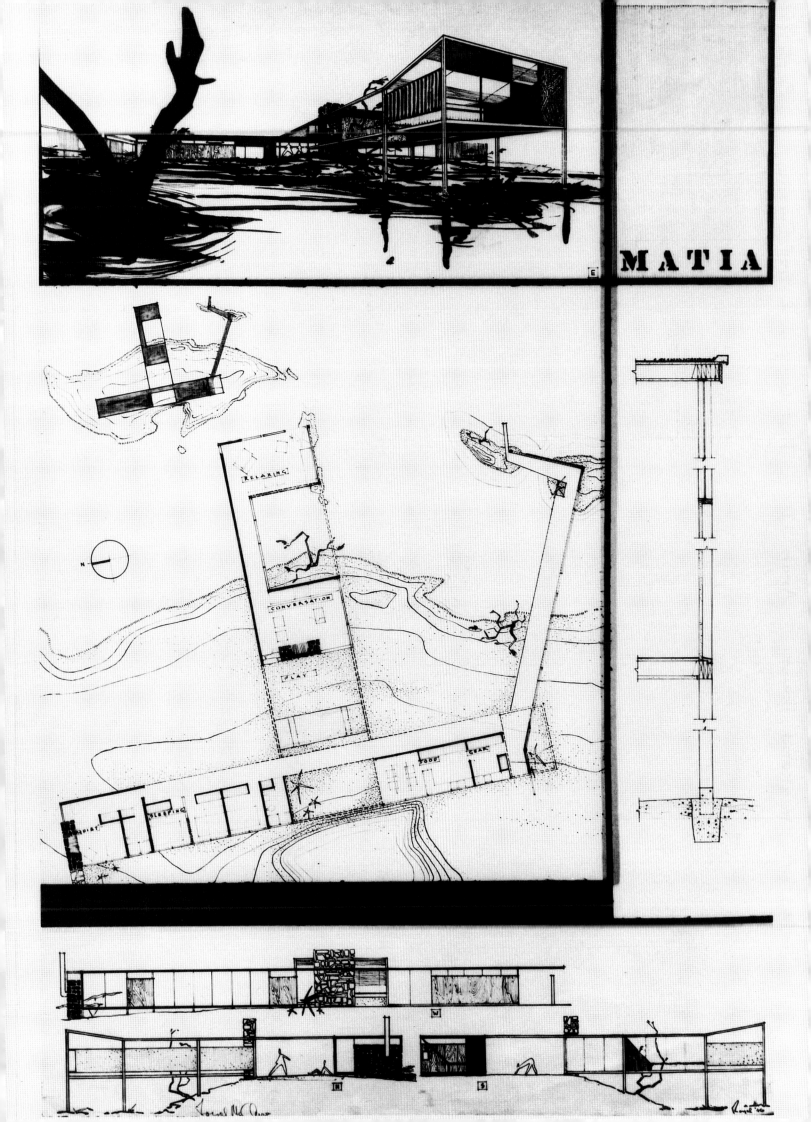

MATIA

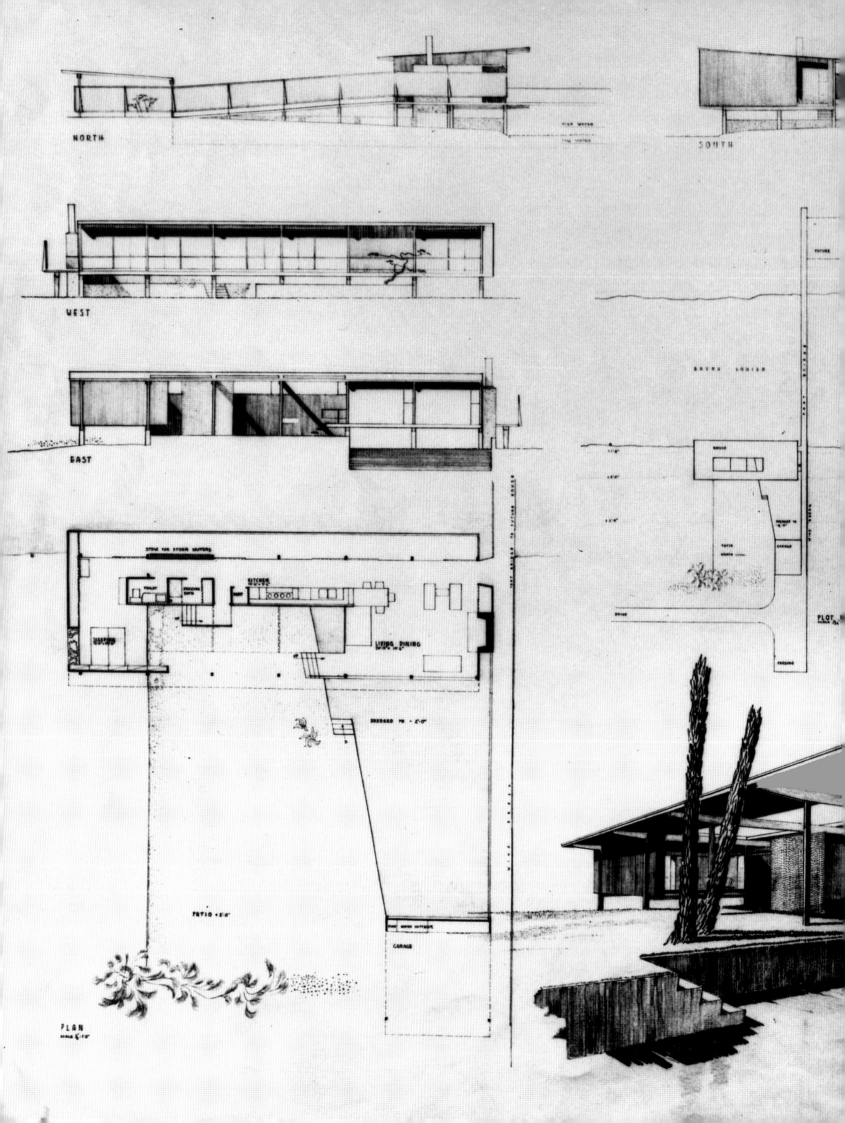

NORTH

SOUTH

WEST

EAST

PLAN

PLOT

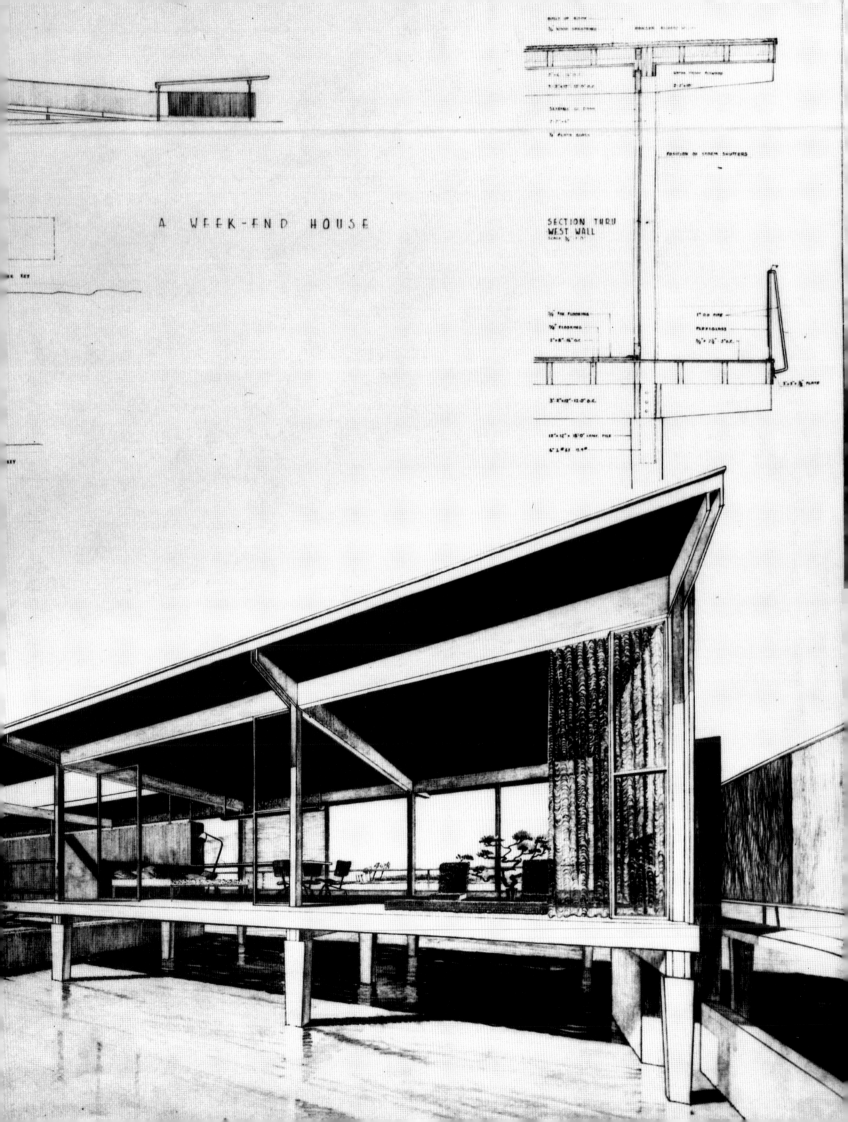

A WEEK-END HOUSE

SECTION THRU
WEST WALL

FALL OPTIONS

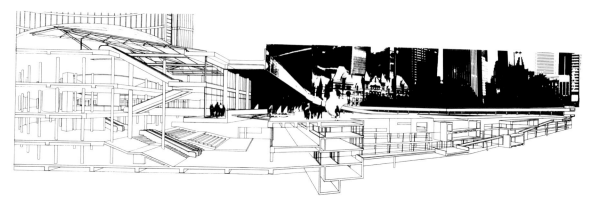

On the Possibility of Public Life in the Post-Industrial City: A Studio Exploration

George Baird

G. Ware Travelstead Professor of Architecture

This design studio focused on the possibility of public life in the post-industrial city. The studio challenged many of the pessimistic critiques of urban public life that have recently been put forward by prominent critics and theorists, and sought, instead, to formulate positive design proposals.

The site of the studio was a public square in front of the City Hall in Toronto, Canada, which has for some years now been considered ripe for redesign and renovation, even though its design is the result of an international competition in 1958. The program material for use in the studio was that which had actually been proposed for the redesign.

The conceptual work of the studio followed three themes:

1. To conceive an architecture of public life appropriate to the contemporary city: students were invited to formulate designs that reflect contemporary theories of public life, accommodating the everyday as much as the ceremonial, the contestatory as well as the congenial, the different as well as the communal.

2. To reinterpret, both critically and imaginatively, urban design principles of the 1950s and 1960s. The existing square and its urban surroundings incorporate two urban design ideas of the 1950s and 1960s to facilitate pedestrian/vehicular segregation: an underground public walkway system and an above-grade pedestrian system. As they approach the existing City Hall, neither of these systems works successfully, and they must be extensively rethought.

3. To reinterpret the symbolism of an existing public building that is only partially successful architecturally, but that has nevertheless become a public icon: the Toronto City Hall. Designed by Finnish architect Viljo Rewell, it is a notable example of the expressionist architecture of the late 1950s, which also includes Eero Saarinen's TWA Terminal at Kennedy Airport and Jørn Utzon's Opera House in Sydney, Australia. Students were asked to develop appropriate means to enhance the setting of this somewhat problematic icon, while recognizing, at the same time, its widespread iconographic popularity.

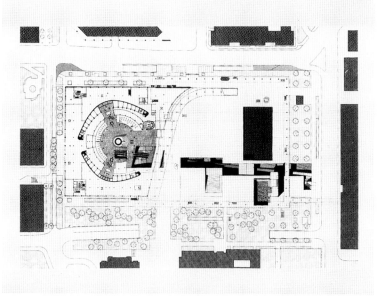

Pablo Savid-Buteler MArch '99, Section, Model View, and Plan

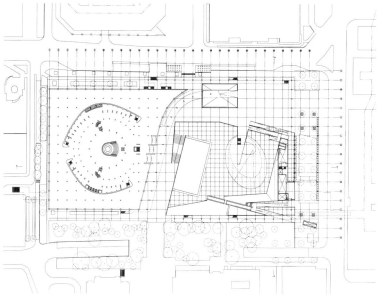

Ho San Chang MArch '99, Ground Level Floor Plan

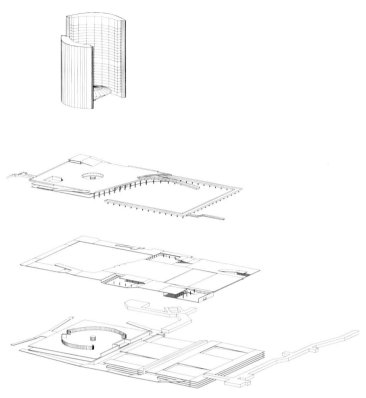

Martin Ibarlucia MAUD '98, Axonometric View

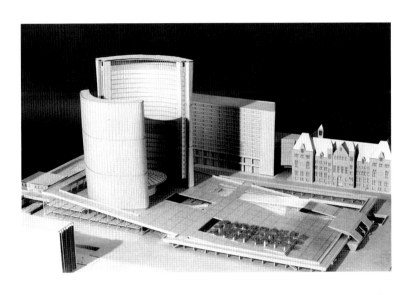

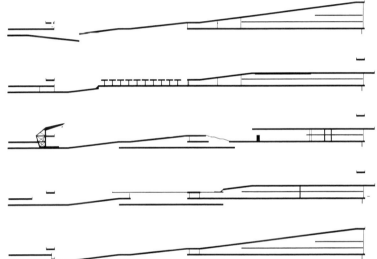

Martin Prominski MLA '98, Model View and Sections

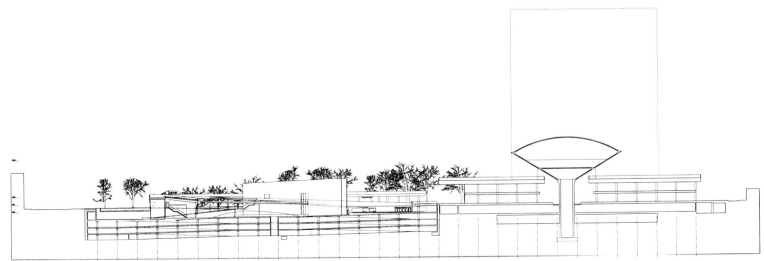

Ho San Chang MArch '99, Longitudinal Section

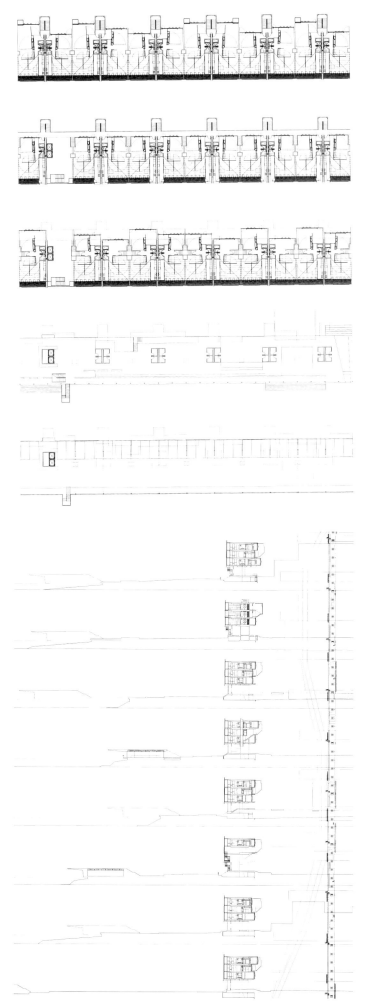

Unsettled City, Unhomely Home

Carol Burns
Associate Professor of Architecture

This studio used housing to look at conditions of the contemporary city, testing the hypothesis that contradictions within these conditions are creating new fields of action for architects and planners. "Contemporary city" refers not to the modern metropolis, but to the city as built out at the end of the financial boom of the 1980s. A new form of human settlement, this city is evolving from reliance on industrial economies to dependence on global business and communications technology. It has evolved from a city rooted in local conditions to a city networked in a system of global city regions, from an entity whose fabric can be described topographically and morphologically to an entity that must also be described as a system of effects whose conditions are perceived as ephemeral. Use-oriented social logics of continuity, location, and tradition cede to exchange-oriented logics of post-industrial capitalism. Processes of urbanization, previously considered controllable, exist today in a state of continuous flux.

Spaces opened up by the decanting of the new low-density American city represent a zone of architectural opportunity. Boundaries continue to exist here, not only in the quantifiable voids of disused harbors and other transport interchanges, but also in buildings, streets, foyers, and parking lots. Admitting that interest in urbanism has been directly proportional to loss of control over urban form, the studio set up a framework for confronting paradoxes in cities. In particular, it explored the relationship between the familiar and the strange—the homely and the unhomely—and examined the role of architecture as an instrument for its physical manifestation.

That which belongs to house and home is familiar, not strange. A sense of security and stability relates to the idea of homelike, or "homely." Contemporary discourses on dwelling attest to the need to seek settledness and rootedness. Even so, ever-changing elements of modernity no longer oppose but become the fundamental reality of one's context, no matter whether one lives in modernist, traditional, or pseudo-traditional physical settings. As pieces of the low-density twentieth-century no longer connect to the city center, residential areas anchor quotidian experience of the city à la carte.

This studio explored the everyday environment of residential settlements in an effort to identify a matching spatial form to the processes and events of the contemporary city and to find a connection between traditional urban fragments, void areas, and recent developments. This emerging city offers territorial solutions and typological programs neither imagined nor supported within the traditional city model.

The studio sequence included three independent projects related to the study area, the Greenpoint section of Brooklyn along the East River. The first project explored and summarized a sequence of regional plans for the New York metropolitan area, as an introduction to city history and to a range of representational techniques. The second short project, construction of an artifact as a means of visual thinking, described relationships among the global market economy, regional culture, and specific local conditions. The final design project addressed housing for 1000 people.

The Joint Center for Housing Studies sponsored the studio, including travel for students and the teaching assistance of Charlie Cannon.

Andrew Junhoe Ku MArch '99, Plans and Sections

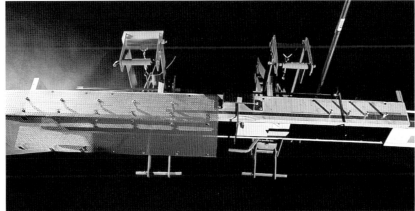

Andrew Junhoe Ku MArch '99, View of Site and Model Views

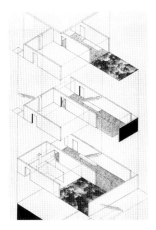
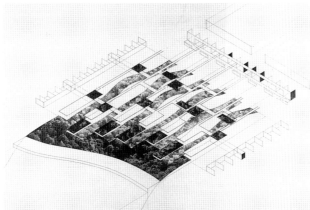

Cedric Perrenoud ETH Exchange, Axonometric Views and Plan

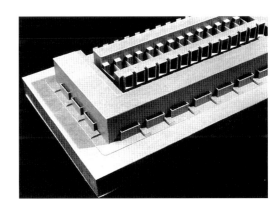

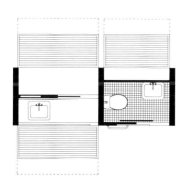
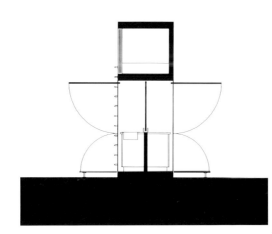
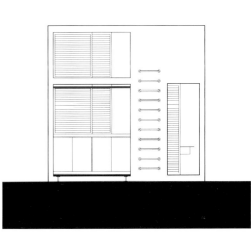

Takashi Yanai MArch '99, Model View, Plan, Section, and Elevation

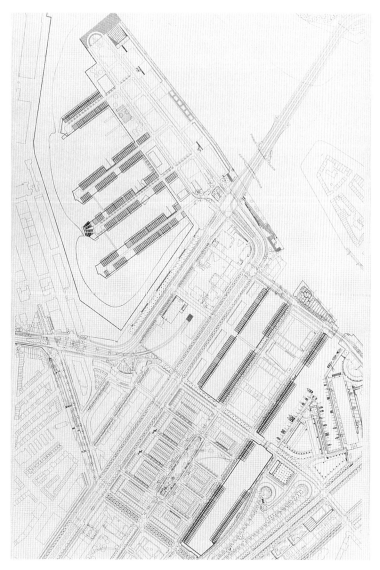

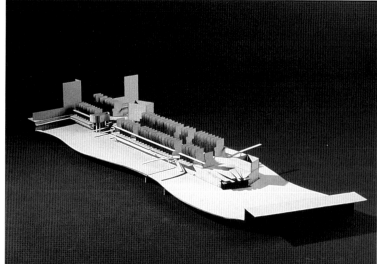

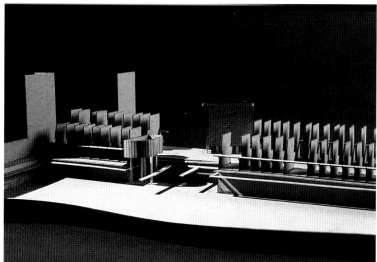

Lindsay Smith MArch '99, Site Plan and Model Views

New Urban Strategies for the Old Port in Rotterdam

Joan Busquets
Visiting Design Critic in Urban Planning and Design

Harbor redevelopment has been a key issue for urban projects during the last two decades. In fact, container development and the increase in ship dimensions has made the old harbor obsolete, and possibilities for reuse are difficult. Consequently, large central spaces became "terrain vague" or derelict land asking for new uses. There is a great deal of experience in North America and Europe that allows a critical discussion of ways to enhance specific features for each continent.

The studio's site was in the port of Rotterdam, where major transformations have left room for new proposals on the left bank of the Maas river. The Kop van Zuid project establishes clear strategies for the redevelopment of the city's southern region, which throughout the city's history has been a place for the harbor and workers. A changing urban ecology demands huge efforts, and major infrastructural changes have already been carried out. Recent waterfront developments in Barcelona, Marseilles, Genoa, and London in Europe and New York, San Francisco, and Toronto in North America were used as reference models to enhance the discussion of new urban strategies.

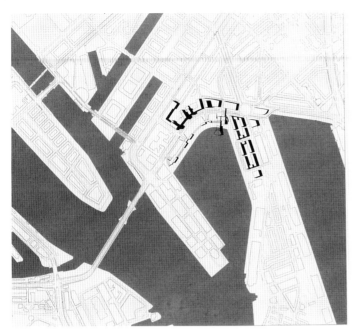
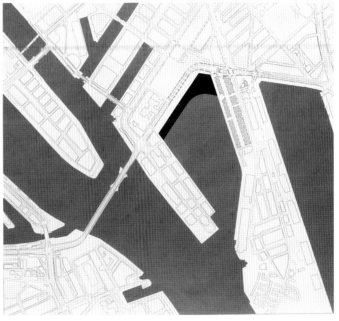

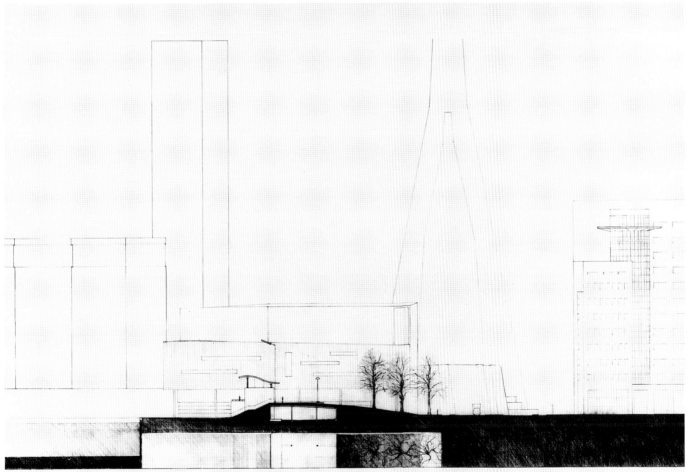

Steven Wilson MAUD '98, Plans and Section

Transforming the Villa La Foce

Gary Hilderbrand
Assistant Professor of Landscape Architecture

Holly Getch Clarke
Design Critic in Landscape Architecture

This studio was based on the proposal to establish a Center for Environmental Planning at Villa La Foce, a 3,000-hectare property in the Val d'Orcia, south of Siena, in the Tuscany region of Italy. The Center would facilitate international exchange and research in practical, theoretical, and management issues related to human occupation of land. La Foce contains important Etruscan ruins, a sixteenth-century manor house, a large farm complex or *fattoria* once comprising some fifty farmsteads, significant gardens, a cemetery, a castle, and the remains of vast land reclamation practices that are currently the focus of ecological study at the University of Florence.

The studio program included live/work space for individual researchers; seminar spaces; and studio/laboratory spaces for design investigations by university students on site. As a point of departure, students examined two important historical typologies of space: the studiolo, exemplified by the private study of the Duke of Montefeltro in Urbino or by the Gubbio Studiolo; and the humanist garden, as defined by the Quattrocento Academy of Lorenzo il Magnifico in Fiesole or the palazzo of Pius II Piccolomini at Pienza. Students then sought to define and develop contemporary landscape equivalents for these paradigms of the cultivated intellectual life. The studio considered the impacts of new intervention on historic fabric both as a source of critical design expression and as ethical praxis, where design proposals become part of a reasoned argument for enlivened contemporary use of cultural resources.

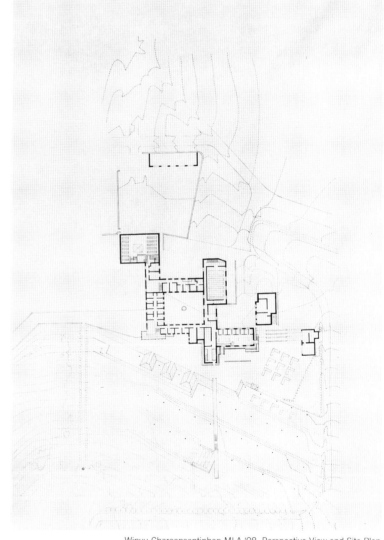

Winyu Charoensantiphap MLA '98, Perspective View and Site Plan

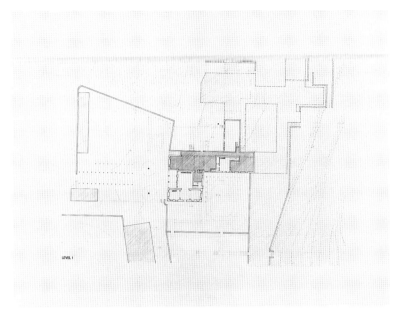

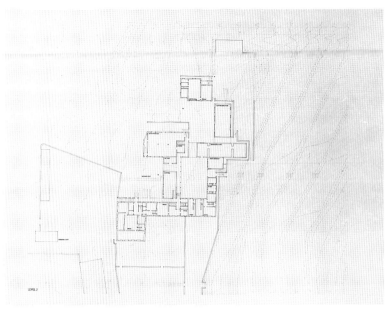

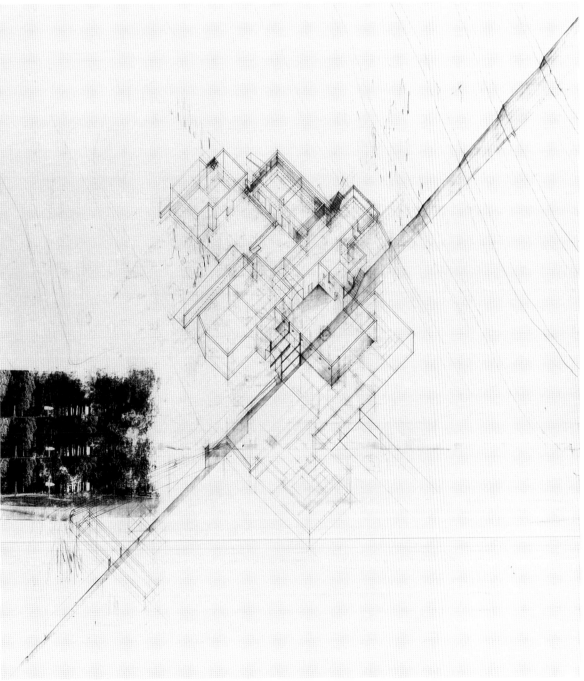

Ke Zhang MArch '98, Level One Plan, Level Two Plan, and Axonometric View

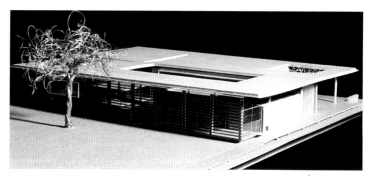

Multipurpose Center at the Menil Collection Museum, Houston, Texas

Carlos Jimenez

Eliot Noyes Visiting Design Critic in Architecture

The studio explored the building of place in residual spaces within the contemporary city—spaces that typically are surrounded by multiple scales of voided and built mass, a common condition in Houston (the fourth largest American city and the largest without zoning). The project did not aim to produce architectures as either immediate or exacerbated renditions of contemporary events (best suited to more agile and ephemeral media), but rather to pursue architectures that confront the building of place in time. To best illustrate the critical potential of this awareness, the Menil Collection Museum district in Houston was chosen as an ideal context for the project.

The Menil Collection Museum is one of the most successful museums constructed in the last two decades. Designed by Renzo Piano (1981-86), the museum occupies a city block within what is primarily a residential enclave, insightfully cultivated through the years as an urban village by John and Dominique de Menil. This village, dedicated to the study, display, and preservation of art, is composed of various wood-framed houses and a set of small buildings that have been either appropriated or built for a specific program: the Rothko Chapel (1971), the Twombly Gallery (1995), and the Byzantine Chapel (1997) are the most architecturally singular of these. As the largest structure within this ensemble of diverse buildings, the museum occupies the symbolic center. The most exemplary characteristic of the Menil ensemble is the way its various fragments have been integrated into an organic and cohesive whole, while maintaining a continual motion (additions, alterations, insertions) as if these were part of a planned strategy and process. Ultimately, what is most interesting about this particular area of the city is that architecture and landscape establish a complicit edification of a larger territory in time, rather than solely emphasizing the singularity of any one building.

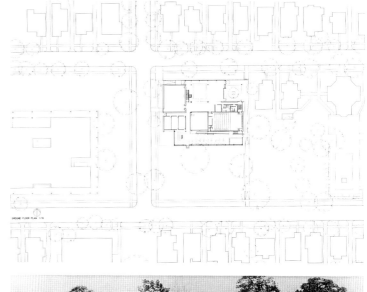

The studio project itself entailed the design of an 18,000–square–foot multipurpose center adjacent to the Menil Museum. The site is a partially wooded half block located to the southeast of the Museum. The purpose of the building is to house a variety of functions (administration offices, auditorium, bookstore, event spaces, and temporary gallery spaces) that are presently housed in the bungalows surrounding the Museum.

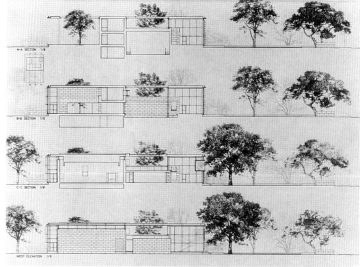

The principal concerns of the studio were: (1) the role(s) that an arts and humanities institution such as the Menil can play in building and continuing local and global cultures; (2) the investigation of urban and suburban relationships or directives already present within the campus-like Menil complex of building(s); (3) the careful placement and integration of a building(s) within the intricate landscape of the site; (4) private and public space determinants in the project's conceptual framework; and (5) the discussion of materials, their selection, and detailing, as a means to amplify each design's intent and resolution.

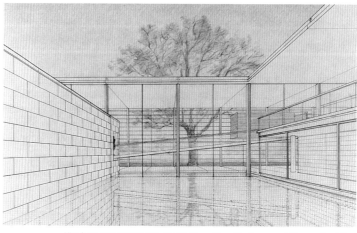

Xiaofeng Zhu MArch '99, Model View, Plan, Sections, and Perspective View

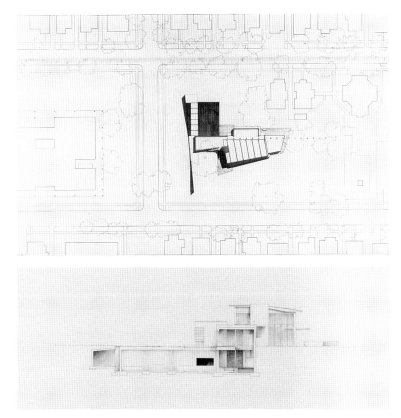

Malcolm Berg MArch '99, Plan, Analytical Model View, Section, and Model View

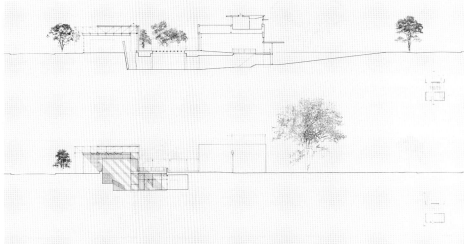

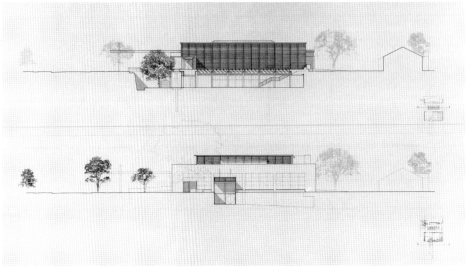

Edward S. Eglin MArch '99, Model View and Sections

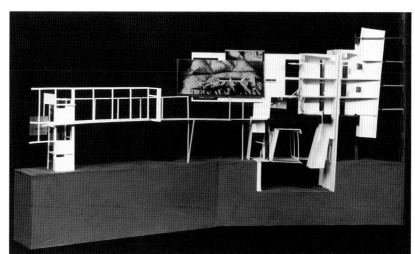

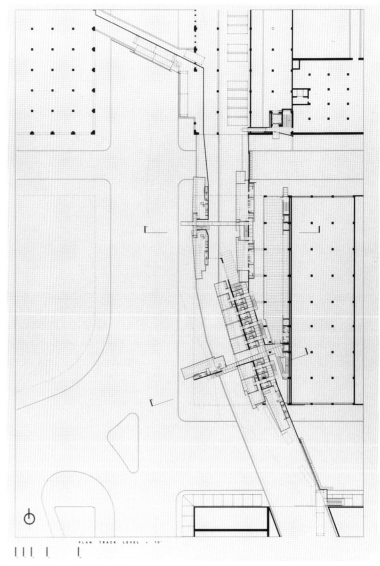

Manhattan East-West: Thresholds of Domesti-City

Sandro Marpillero

Visiting Design Critic in Architecture

Experience of urban thresholds is becoming less recognizable. In the words of Walter Benjamin, "falling asleep is perhaps the only such experience that has remained to us (and with it, though, also awakening)."

Students pursued the design of thresholds in both their tectonic and ceremonial aspects, through the interpretation of existing sites and the projection of modes of inhabitation. Relying on the students' familiarity with the technical aspects of housing design, we re-examined the notion of domesti-city at three scales of operation: the dwelling unit, the building, and the site. We worked with transitions between these scales, and between an individual and the city.

The studio focused on the emergence of architectural figures, through three modes of design representation: (1) documenting how elements are condensed into a collage's depth; (2) interpreting how identities can be captured from within a section's plane; and (3) conceiving models that deploy traces of either of the above operations, and produce figural distortions. By using these "techniques of invention," students became aware of how figures interact and oscillate between different spatial dimensions.

The first part of the semester was spent mapping intersections and tensions in two urban conditions that are located at the eastern and western edges of 14th Street in Manhattan. The eastern site faces Brooklyn; its fabric of modernist "towers in the green" is dominated by the stack of a power plant, and overlooks a highway that prevents access to a waterfront park. The western site faces New Jersey through a landscape of decaying piers; its fabric of industrial warehouses is pierced by an abandoned elevated railway line and is currently undergoing a process of accelerated rehabilitation for high-end commercial and residential uses. Each student chose one site and selected among the thresholds identified which one to modify in order to construct spaces for inhabitation.

Sven Oliver Schroeter MArch '99, Section of
Elevated Tracks, Model View, and Plan of Housing Units

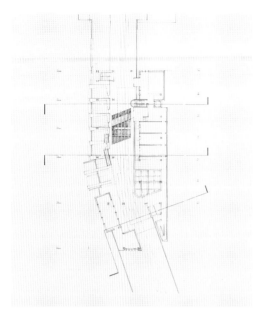

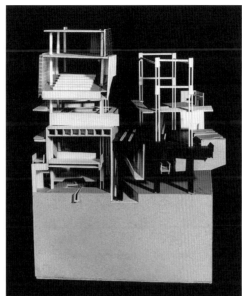

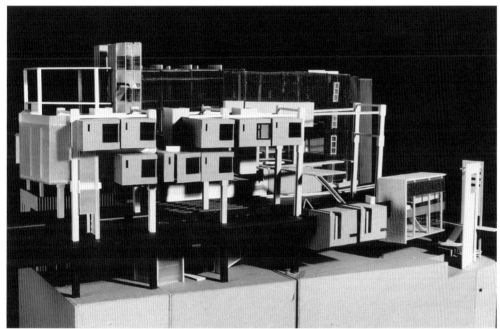

Sanki Choe MArch '99, Upper Level Plan and Model Views

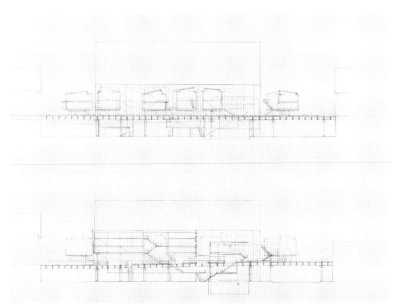

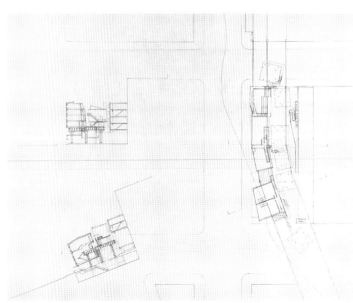

Anthony Piermarini MArch '99, Longitudinal Sections, and Elevated Rail Plan and Cross Sections

Marked Down: Detroit and the Mortification of Memory

Peter Rose

Adjunct Professor of Architecture

Hard times here with me now,
Hard times here with me now,
If they don't get no better,
I believe I'll leave this town.

"Hard Times," Floyd James, 1948

This studio focused on the City of Detroit, one-time "Arsenal of Democracy," which at its zenith epitomized the success of urban industrial America, but now stands as the principal symbol of post-war urban decline.

Detroit's history is inseparable from modernity's meta-narratives of memory and forgetting that run through our century. It is inseparable from the destruction that modernity wreaked on memory by dismantling nineteenth-century urban perceptions and invigorating present life with self-conscious newness. Detroit's history sprang from modernity's celebration of the future as liberating progress over and against the burdens of the past.

In Detroit, industry and commerce succeeded at unprecedented rates, generating broad new middle classes freed from the constraints of the past. Detroit was a radical attempt to humiliate history into submission by creating a material plenitude so vast it would make the past irrelevant. The city's successes seemed to prove Henry Ford's dictum: history was bunk.

When this exhilarating idea ran out of gas, it left Detroit and its people vulnerable. The automobile revolution that fueled Detroit's rise also forged a bourgeois ambition to escape the city for the suburbs. Since 1950, middle-class flight has systematically emptied the city of its human and material substance. Subsequently, a quarter of a million buildings have been razed; between 1970 and 1987 the city averaged a net loss of fourteen residential structures every day.

Detroit is now witnessing signs of rebirth. However, recent efforts to rebuild have been accompanied by a deep anxiety about the city's past. Residents of the city now face, in addition to breathtaking physical and social disintegration, the legacy of the city it once was. The history of this city is an extraordinary representational project, delineating a rise, a fall, and an uncertain future. The burdens of the past are palpable; Detroit is a city that feels humiliated by its history.

The studio explored problems of memory and history in Detroit through the vehicle of Hudson's, once the nation's largest department store. Established in 1881, Hudson's grew to occupy a full city block, boasting no fewer than 40 acres of floor space, before closing its doors in 1983. Now that the mega-retailer has followed its patrons to the suburbs, its former headquarters stands empty and vandalized. Recently acquired by the city, the building is slated for destruction not for functional reasons so much as symbolic ones. The city's mortification has led some to believe that its recent past must be repressed, eradicated, and treated as dead and unthinkable.

Challenging this willful amnesia under the belief that we forget at our own peril, the studio explored possibilities for bringing the Hudson's building back to life. Work on tectonic study models preceded an examination of the building, where programmatic concerns included commercial, residential, and public spaces as well as the very real concern of surplus space. Christopher Agosta was the teaching assistant for the studio.

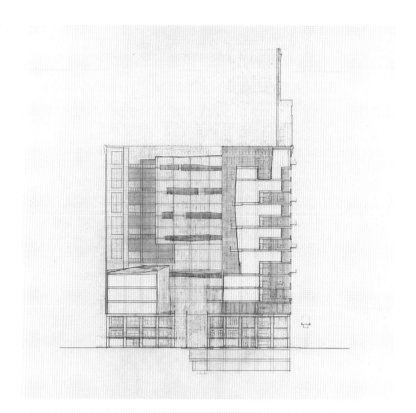

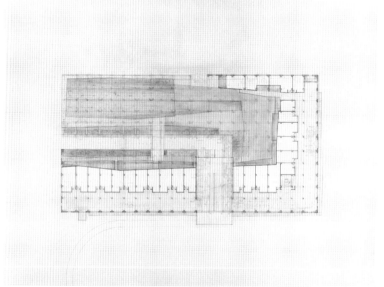

Christina Long MArch '99, Section, Plan, and Tectonic Study Models

Michelle Kim MArch '99, Model View

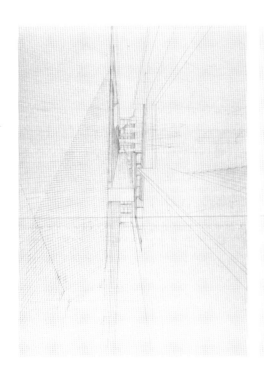

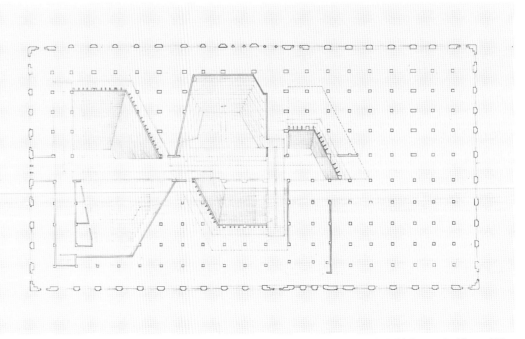

Sang-Won Lee MArch '99, Perspective View and Plan

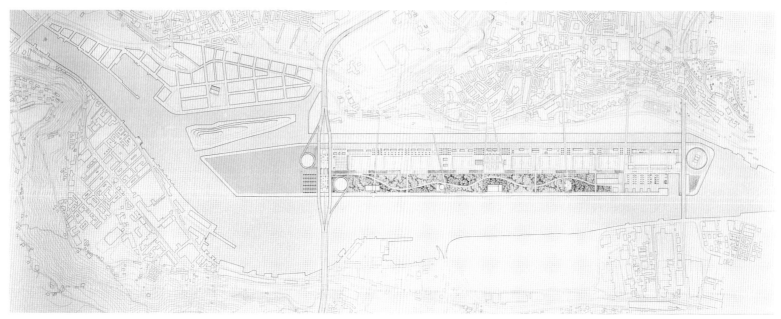

Christian Dagg MArch '99 and Carie Penabad MAUD '98, Plan

La Ria de Bilbao

Jorge Silvetti
Nelson Robinson, Jr., Professor of Architecture

Rodolfo Machado
Professor in Practice of Architecture and Urban Design

This sponsored studio, jointly offered by the departments of Architecture and Urban Planning and Design, focused on the ria de Bilbao, on the northern coast of Spain. The ria de Bilbao, the 3-kilometer-long deep-sea inlet where the city of Bilbao (the economic and financial capital of the Basque region) and its old harbor are located, saw an unplanned and rapid development of heavy industry (steel mills and shipyards) along both banks that had traditionally been the domain of the fishing industry. The 1980s economic crisis, together with the appearance of global markets and the loss of competitiveness of the industry, meant a progressive deterioration of all of this infrastructure. In a positive attempt to recover its place as the most important port of the peninsula and one of the most important Atlantic harbors in Europe, a new state-of-the-art harbor facility was built outside the ria.

Today, Bilbao stands at the beginning of a spectacular process of development aimed at recovering its leading role in Spanish economic and cultural spheres, with its urban territory in need of transformation. Emblematic of this re-launching of this city's central role are the acclaimed Guggenheim Museum by Frank Gehry on the ria's most central location and the new subway system designed by Sir Norman Foster. Essential to the continuity of this process will be the 'recovery' of its ria, now containing the ruins of an impressive industrial landscape and many still undeveloped areas. The studio, which was sponsored by the Diputacion Foral de Bizkaia (the highest regional authority) and is part of a larger research project, was followed by the spring-semester studio conducted by Jorge Silvetti and Francisco Mangado. The fall-semester studio concentrated on the area of the city of Barakaldo to study its recovery and new development potential both at the architectural and urban design scales. The studio was ideal for students with a strong interest in urban issues, urban programming, public spaces, and medium to large-scale architectural interventions, as well as redevelopment of industrial and waterfront areas.

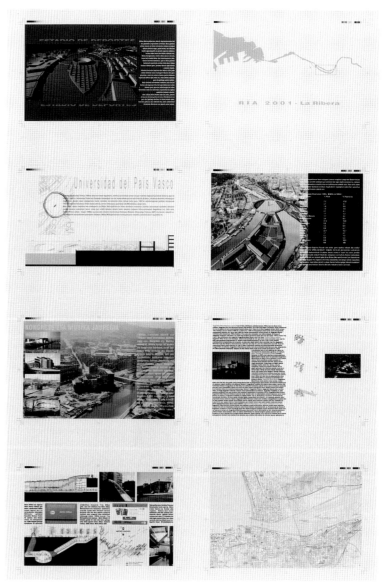

Jonathan Hoover MArch '99 and John Lee MAUD '98, Project Page Layouts

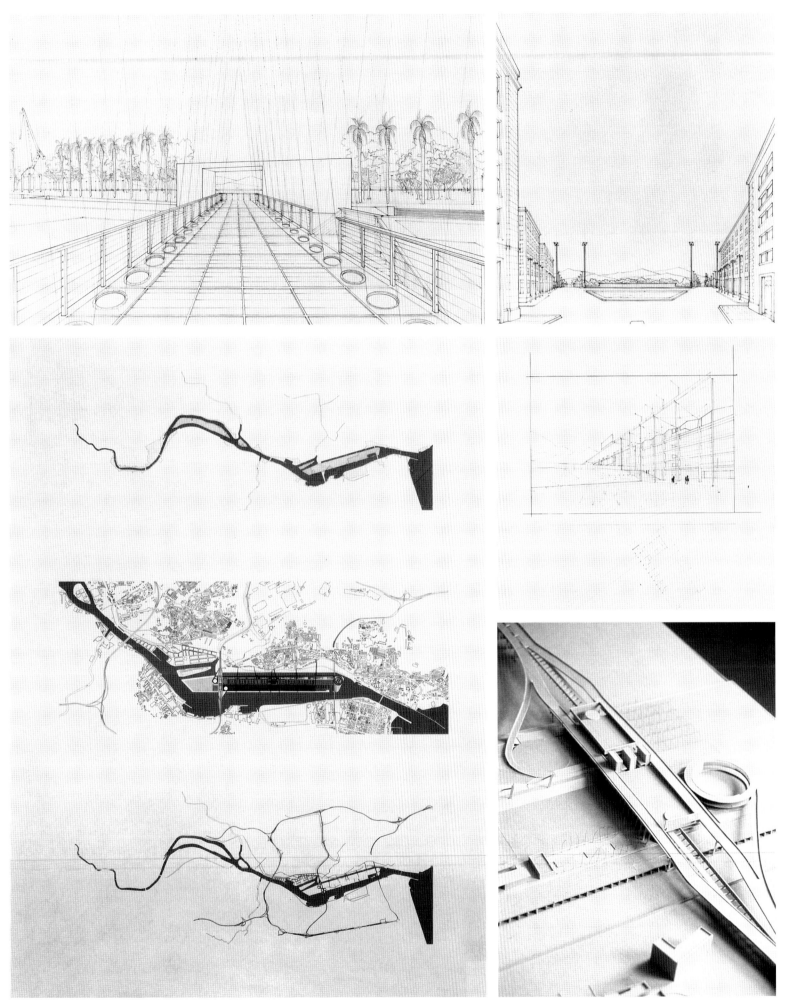

Christian Dagg MArch '99 and Carie Penabad MAUD '98, Perspective Views, Analysis Diagrams, and Model View

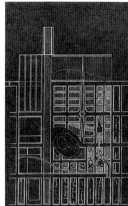

Maria I. Nardi MLA '98, Model View and Site Plan

Design Visions/Political Realities

Ken Smith
Design Critic in Landscape Architecture

Rebecca Robertson
Visiting Design Critic in Urban Planning and Design

The basic notion of this studio was that grand urban visions are creative not only in their design but in their implementation, and that the best realized urban plans are those that integrate design vision with equally creative tactics to get them done. The students were asked to design a project that would have a significant effect on New York City, and to take the project through a political process, in which lobbying, influence-peddling, offering "sweeteners," and arguing the case on the merits were all acceptable tactics.

The project area encompassed forty blocks in Manhattan between Herald Square, Times Square, and the Hudson River. Today it is a complex yet indistinct urban landscape, dominated by the Javits Convention Center, Penn Station, the under-utilized railyards, the Port Authority Bus Terminal, and the Lincoln Tunnel bridges and ramps. Because it contains numerous "soft sites," and because of its proximity to major transportation, Herald Square, the developing Hudson River Park, and the newly revitalized Times Square and 42nd Street, this area will probably undergo an intensive transformation in the early part of the next century. In recent years, it has been the subject of many proposals, including a relocated Yankee Stadium, expansion of the Convention Center, a new Madison Square Garden, a new hotel district, a new entertainment district, and relocation of Penn Station into the Farley Post Office Building.

The studio focused on developing compelling urban visions within the context of a realpolitik. Students were asked to design projects that would create significant "places" in the city, accompanied by realistic strategies for implementation. As part of the studio's work, the students also role-played as political constituencies representing City Hall, the local community, an influential citywide civic group, the real estate board, etc. The constituencies developed positions on the projects and the project proponents attempted to work through them. The studio was accompanied by discussions of relevant case studies such as Central Park, 42nd Street, Westway/Hudson River Park, and Columbus Circle, where grand public visions and political realities came together with varying results.

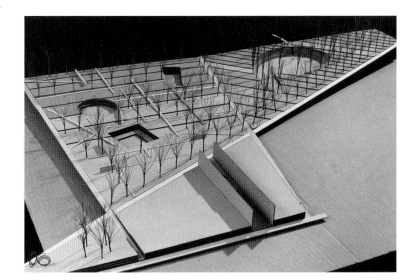

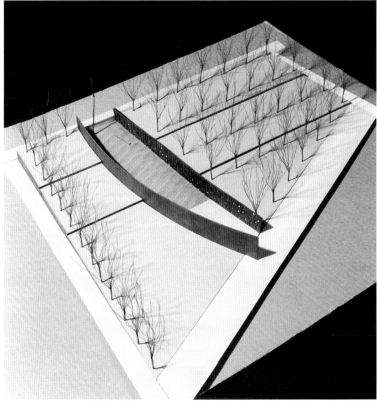

Claudia Taborda MLA "99, Model Views

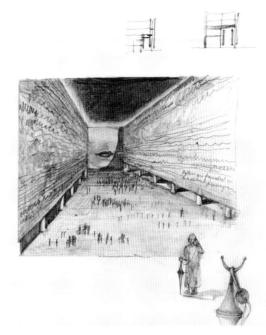

Maria I. Nardi MLA '98, Context Plan and Perspective Views of New York World's Fair of 2020

North - South Spine Plan
Growth Stage 1

■ Existing Protected Areas
■ Proposed Nature Reserves
■ Proposed Agriculture Reserves
■ Rural Open Space
■ Streams
■ Existing Built Areas
■ Settlement Growth
■ Commercial
■ Institutional
■ Industrial
■ Powerlines
■ Roads

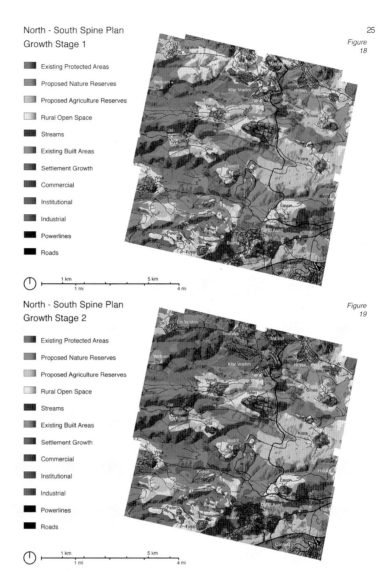

1 km 5 km
1 mi 4 mi

North - South Spine Plan
Growth Stage 2

Figure
19

■ Existing Protected Areas
■ Proposed Nature Reserves
■ Proposed Agriculture Reserves
■ Rural Open Space
■ Streams
■ Existing Built Areas
■ Settlement Growth
■ Commercial
■ Institutional
■ Industrial
■ Powerlines
■ Roads

1 km 5 km
1 mi 4 mi

Alternative Futures in the Western Galilee, Israel

Carl Steinitz

*Alexander and Victoria Wiley Professor
of Landscape Architecture and Planning*

This sponsored studio focused on a part of the Galilee in northern Israel. Stef Wertheimer is the sponsor of the studio. His group of companies, ISCAR, is Israel's leading "high tech" manufacturing and exporting company in machine tools and plastics. Wertheimer strongly believes that commercial arrangements among entrepreneurs are the key to long-lasting peace in the region, and being a "doer," he wants to help make this happen.

His central concept is the sponsorship of Zur University and its affiliated "incubator industry." The school is an international institute for entrepreneurs in manufacturing open to students from all of the Mediterranean and Middle East. It was founded in temporary quarters in 1994 and is to be located on a hill at Lavon, along with housing and "incubator industry" facilities. The curriculum is being developed by the MIT Sloan School of Management and the Harvard Business School.

The studio proposed alternatives for the future development and conservation of the 100 sq. km. area which is the context of the large Wertheimer land holdings. It includes several Arab, Druze, and Jewish villages and nature reserves, industrial parks, and a new town. The studio also designed alternatives for the Lavon site, including a new Zur University and the expansion of the Tefen Industrial Municipality.

The studio was not "one student-one design." Rather, it was organized, after a site visit, by the class as one large, multidisciplinary collaborative, whose task was to identify and design options for the doubling of industrial production and the quadrupling of population. For further description of the studio see:
http://gsd.harvard.edu/~iscar/alternative futures/gag.htm.

Studio Participants:

Guillemette de Boucaud MArch '99, Alan Jay Christensen MDesS '98, Jerry Coburn MDesS '98, Thomas Cody MUP '98, Christine Dianni MLA '98, Michael Flaxman DDes '00, David Hofmann MArch '99, Seon Hee Jung MArch '99, Laurie Malin MLA '98, Baker Mallory MArch/MLA '99, Amir Mueller MLA '98, Francis Reiner MLA '98, Christy Rogers MLA '98, Krista Schneider MLA '98, Sharon Tepper MUP '98, Vardit Tsurnamal MLA '99, Dena Zyroff MArch '99, with John Felkner DDes '99

North-South Spine Plans: Growth Stage 1 and 2; Computer Rendering of Lavon High Density Alternative, looking south; Computer Rendering of Lavon High-Density Alternative: Shared University and Civic Facilities

Computer Rendering of Community Tefen with Mixed-use Boulevard, Looking Southwest; and Computer Rendering of Lavon High-Density Alternative, Looking North

Katherine Bennett MLA '99, Model View

Maximum Return: Problems of Order, Economy, and Change

Marc Treib

Visiting Design Critic in Landscape Architecture

Landscape architectural order motivated the three projects at the core of the studio, each of them based on the notion of economy and change. Here, economy was understood not as minimal expenditure, but as return on resources utilized. Change included variation over the daily and annual cycles, and over time. For the first project, students found overgrown or heavily planted sites and used selective removal as the basis of design. Project two, in contrast, reconfigured an urban block using a highly-constrained palette and limited amount of landscape materials. The third project, the semester's principal exercise, concerned the design of a plaza/park joining three units of the Museum of New Mexico in Santa Fe. Its method drew on the lessons of the first two exercises.

Jeeun Song MLA '98, Model View and Urban Block Ground Cover

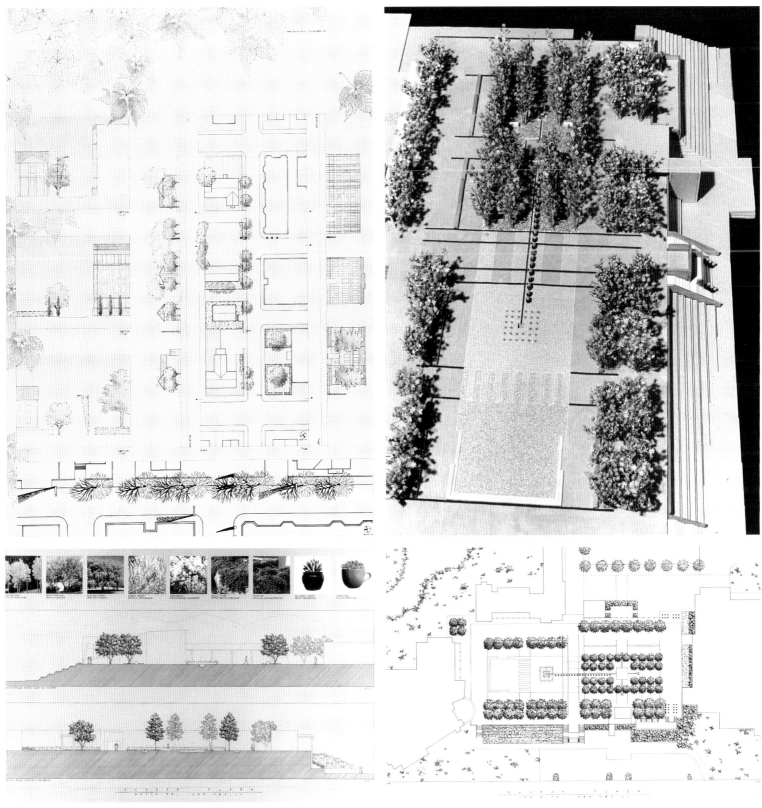

Misty March MLA '99, Site Plan, Model View, Sections, and Plan

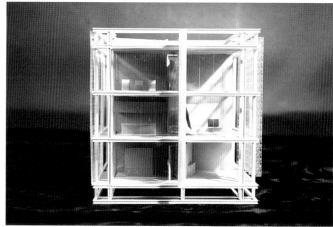

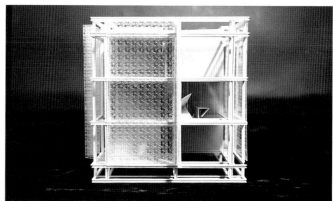

Sum of Parts

Calvin Tsao
Visiting Design Critic in Architecture

Too often, architecture is envisioned mainly as a construct of concepts and polemics, and in practice it is habitually approached from the "macro" working toward the "micro." These approaches have often caused architecture to lose sight of its fundamental purpose: to continually investigate and improve the "built environment," the material surroundings in which humanity lives out its physical and metaphysical existence.

This studio proposed instead that architecture should consider simultaneously all relevant realities about how we live: global, regional, and local contexts; architectonic and internal spatial realities; and finally, but no less importantly, the minute details of function and aesthetics. Thoughtful consideration of the micro issues within each of these realities thus informed and enhanced our consideration of the macro issues. A useful consequence of this process was that the conventional macro-weighted biases became open to fair criticism.

The residence that we designed in this studio—a secluded vacation retreat—was an ideal project with which to investigate our approach. As we wished to focus on the central and universal issues of living and not on individual idiosyncrasies, our residence had not a single user, but many users. They possibly, however, had common interests or desires, which introduced additional dimensions—and additional challenges—to our design exercise.

The studio considered and approached the process of designing our retreat inversely, "from the inside out;" consequently, our starting points were sensibility and sensuality, rather than standard typologies or paradigms. We demonstrated that this approach did not require us to sacrifice imagination, innovation, or meaning.

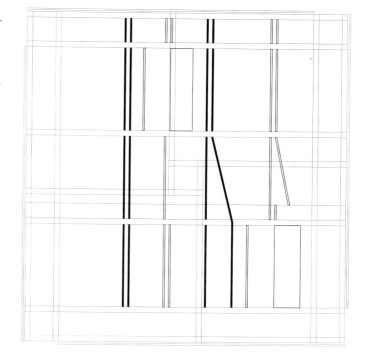

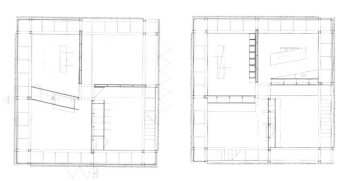

Rebecca G. O'Neal MArch '99, Model Views, Section Profile of Core Walls, and Plans

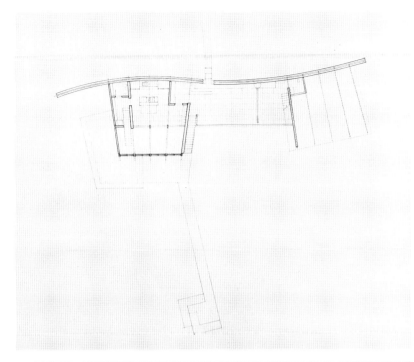

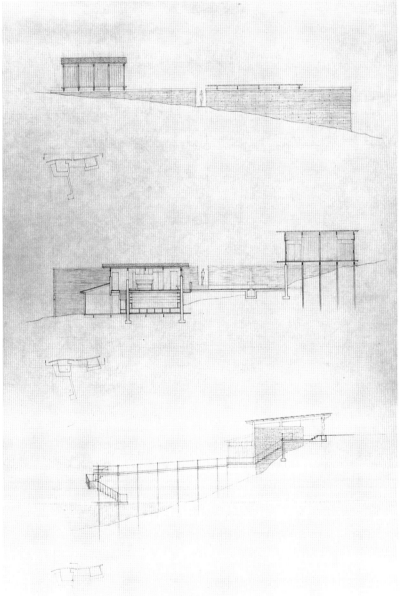

Paul Masi MArch '98, Model Views

Carolyn Straub MArch '99, Plan, Elevation, and Sections

Boston Metropolitan Greenspace Initiative

Robert Yaro

Visiting Design Critic in Urban Planning and Design

This studio assisted the Metropolitan Area Planning Council in developing a new Metropolitan Greenspace Plan for the Boston region continuing a long tradition of GSD leadership in open space and land use planning for the metropolitan area. First, we forecast land use change through the year 2020, and used a Geographic Information System to map likely development trends. We then identified and mapped key natural resource systems and scenic and cultural landscapes in Eastern Massachusetts, including significant ridge lines, river valleys, rare species habitats, agricultural districts, trail corridors, wetland and coastal systems, and other features that should be protected in the first decades of the new century.

We then investigated how this network of protected landscapes could provide a permanent framework for future growth in the metropolitan area. The studio also examined potential public and private actions required to achieve protection of these places, including local, regional, or state land use regulatory measures, and various land acquisition and limited development techniques. Based on this examination we recommended a package of these actions for adoption by the Metropolitan Area Planning Council (MAPC), the Commonwealth, municipalities, and private conservation groups.

Finally, the studio met with environmental and civic leaders and state and municipal officials to gain their input and support for the plan that emerged from this effort. Our client was MAPC, with input from the state Executive Office of Environmental Affairs. The Trustees of Reservations and other private conservation groups also advised the studio. MAPC has already begun the process of developing the plan, and we built on their achievements to date, including a recently completed GIS land use and land use change map of the region.

For more than a century, the Boston region has been a leading innovator in landscape protection and park development. Olmsted's 1876 Boston Parks Plan resulted in the Emerald Necklace, the Nation's first planned urban park system. In 1891 the Trustees of Reservations was established as the world's first land trust. Then, with support from TTOR, Charles Eliot proposed the creation of the metropolitan park system, another first. Finally, Charles Eliot II and Benton MacKaye proposed the creation of the Bay Circuit, a continuous trail and greenbelt in what is now the Route 128 corridor ringing Boston.

However, since World War II the Boston region has lagged in promoting a green vision for its future. Since then, despite only a 14% increase in population, sprawling suburban and exurban growth has consumed 42% of the region's open land, fragmenting wildlife habitat, destroying farm and forest land, and destroying some of the Commonwealth's most cherished scenic and historic landscapes. The Commonwealth of Massachusetts has invested hundreds of millions of dollars in open space protection, and continues to protect thousands of acres of open land every year, but these investments have not been made in the context of a comprehensive, region-wide open space strategy. Environmental Affairs Secretary Trudy Coxe is strongly committed to completing a greenspace plan that can guide these investments in the future.

Across the U.S. and around the world metropolitan regions are adopting metropolitan open space plans in order to shape patterns of development, contain urban sprawl, protect natural areas, and provide needed public access and recreational opportunities. For more than half a century, London's Green Belt has shaped the physical development of southeast England. Paris's new Plan Vert and a network of regional parks will permanently protect important landscapes in the Ile de France Region surrounding France's capital. And several U.S. metropolitan regions, including New York, Chicago, San Francisco, Philadelphia, and Portland, Oregon, are building regional open space networks. Our job was to help MAPC and the Commonwealth learn from these experiences, and build on the rich legacy left by Olmsted, the Eliots, and MacKaye to develop an effective plan for a similar connected regional open space system for metropolitan Boston.

Studio Participants:

Amy Cupples-Rubiano MLA '98, Karla Ebenbach MUP '98, Justin Grigg MLA '98, Mary Leibe MLA '98, Esther Paik MUP '98, Sissy Willis MLA '98, and Thomas Yardley MUP '98

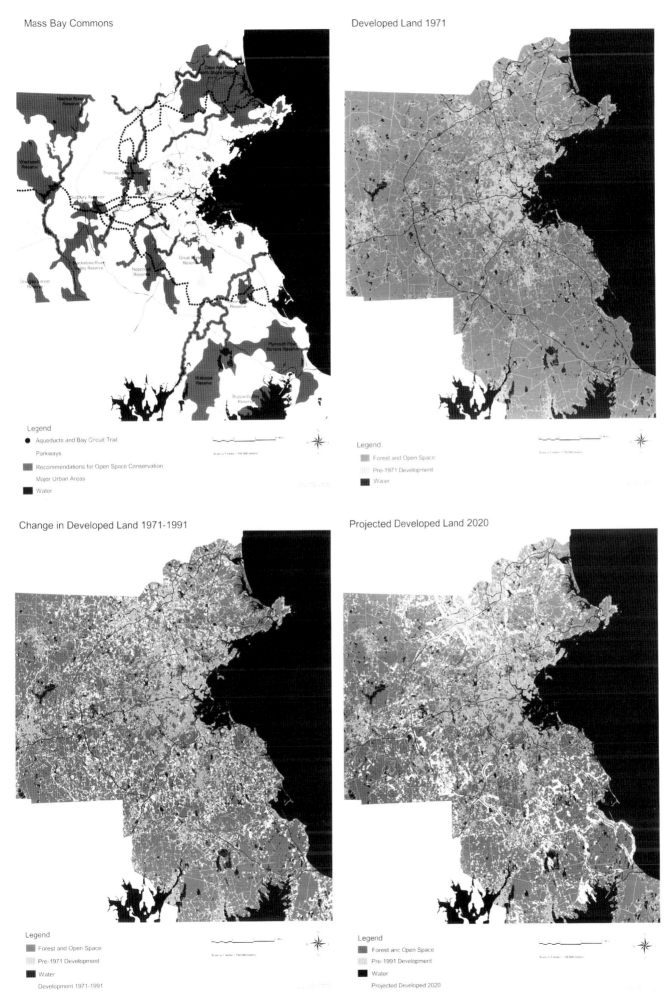

Mass Bay Commons

Developed Land 1971

Legend
- Aqueducts and Bay Circuit Trail
  Parkways
  Recommendations for Open Space Conservation
  Major Urban Areas
  Water

Legend
  Forest and Open Space
  Pre-1971 Development
  Water

Change in Developed Land 1971-1991

Projected Developed Land 2020

Legend
  Forest and Open Space
  Pre-1971 Development
  Water
  Development 1971-1991

Legend
  Forest and Open Space
  Pre-1991 Development
  Water
  Projected Developed 2020

Mass Bay Commons, Developed Land 1971, Change in Developed Land 1971-1991, Projected Developed Land 2020

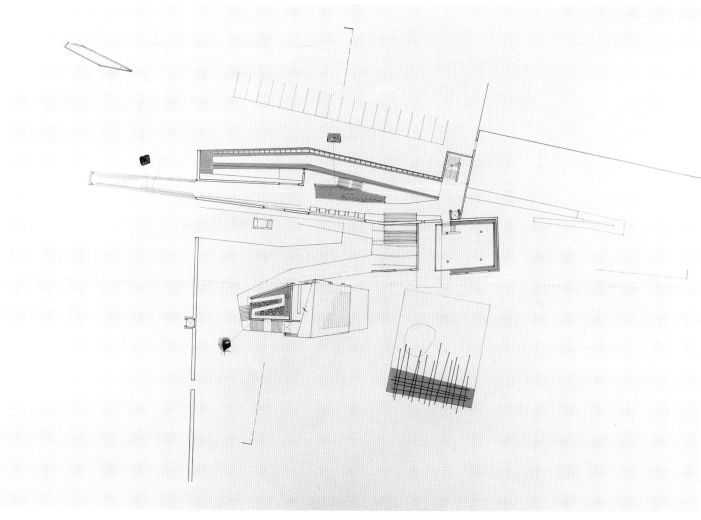

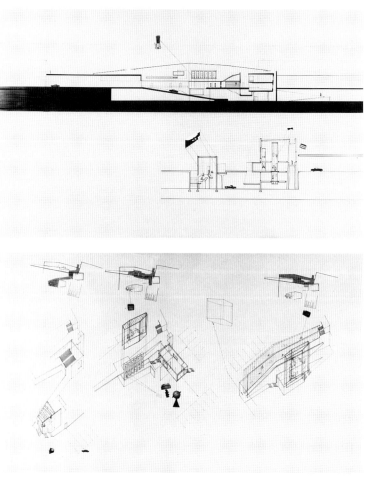

The Ruins of a Shopping Center and a New Museum in the Edge City of Framingham

Mirko Zardini
Visiting Design Critic in Architecture

Parallel to the proliferation of images and the virtual world, the world of objects still provides the setting for a large part of our lives. On one hand this relationship is regulated by the mechanism of shopping, and on the other by an increasing phenomenon of aestheticization. This dichotomy is represented by two typologies: the shopping center and the museum.

The project proposal included designing a museum linked to an existing shopping center. The combination of these two very different elements stimulated an investigation of their specific characteristics: the concept of typology, the idea of container, the character of the buildings, their relationship to exterior spaces, the idea of exhibiting and display, the phenomena of hybridism, and the new centers of the contemporary city.

The project offered an opportunity for reflection on the architecture of today's city, but also on the transformations that seem to be the guiding concept for design.

Elizabeth Whittaker MArch '99, Plan, Sections, and Axonometric Travel Sequence

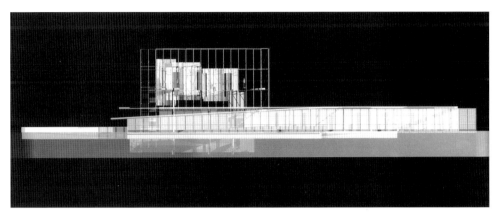

Shane Williamson MArch '99, Front Elevation and View of Display Room

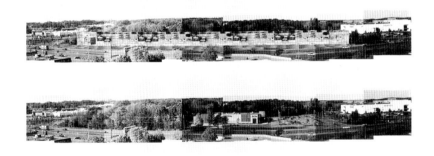

Emiliano Lopez MArch '99, Elevations

SHOPPERS WORLD SCALE MODEL KIT

Congratulations! You have your hands on an authentic replica of the fabulous Shoppers World plaza in Framingham, Massachusetts. To assemble your own superstores, follow the directions included. Then read the pages regarding rules of arrangement, layouts, and compatibility

When you're ready to begin, on a large sheet of paper, arrange your buildings. Then use the parking stencil to draw your parking plan. Add cars, trees, lamps, and anything else you might find in a megamall and have fun. It's your chance to be a world-class real estate developer!

FUTURE RULES OF ARRANGEMENT

If you choose to develop your world into a livelier, denser shopping arena, then follow these rules. Below is a future plan of Shoppers World, Framingham. In this scheme, category-killer stores have taken over the site, replacing former warehouses with themed attraction substores. More warehouses have been built in the place of parking, and multi-level parking structures are carefully attached to courtyards.

Parking requirements

Continue to provide 5 parking spaces for every 1000 square feet. The warehouse buildings are each 40,000 sq.ft., so they would require 200 spaces each. Keep adding levels of parking until you have enough spaces, but do not exceed the height of the warehouses themselves.

Vehicular circulation is now limited to the outer perimeter of the site. Because the parking structures are the only point of entry for cars, pay special attention to the entrances. Mark them with big signs and colors.

Spiral parking structures take the place of surface parking. There should be two elevator/stair banks, on opposite ends. These circulation points should lead directly to shopping.

Pedestrian entrances to the parking structures should be treated with as much care as warehouse entrances.

The parking structures should not abut the warehouses. Leave enough room to form pedestrian paths, connecting the courtyards.

Building Layout

The front of each store should face a courtyard, together forming a small village-like environment.

The rear of each store should be accessible to trucks for loading, away from the courtyards and served by a secondary road. This side of the store should be hidden as much as possible from the main road.

New buildings on the inside should have hidden service entrances embedded in the parking structures.

Again, avoid creating unusable, triangular spaces between buildings. Putting two buildings side by side saves construction costs and simplifies circulation.

Now that the stores are closer together, their signs can be smaller and finely detailed. Each storefront should be detailed to disguise the larger scale of the warehouse.

Courtyards

Allow "cow-paths" to form, marking pedestrian routes as they would naturally develop.

Fill the remaining shapes with grass, trees, and flowers. Allow these patches of greenery to become picnic areas or recreational fields.

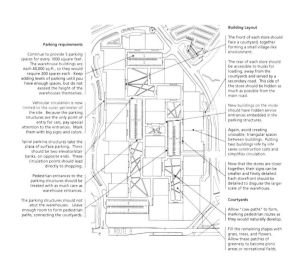

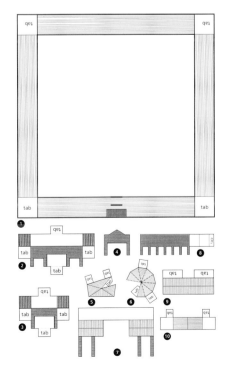

Raymond Chung MArch '99, Children's Game as Site Analysis

School of Harvard University Architecture

TASK

50 cts.

National Planning and Housing Issue

We Have Learned from the War
National Planning
Housing in the Nation's Economy
New Kensington Saga
Experiment in Planning
Policy for Our Cultural Heritage

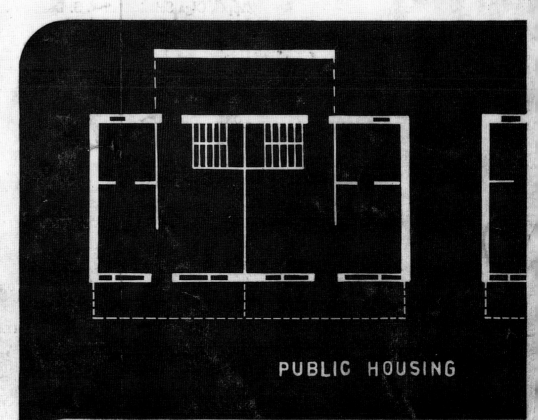
PUBLIC HOUSING

No. 5

50 cts.

SPRING OPTIONS

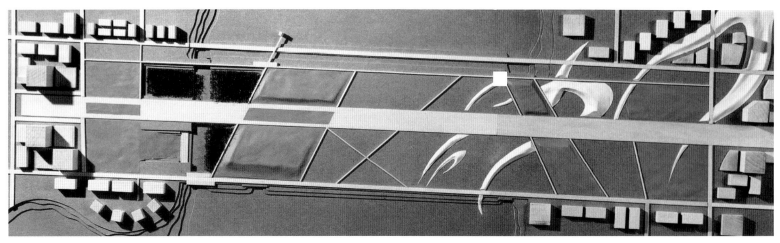

Stapleton Airport Redevelopment:
Ecology + Community, Without Barriers

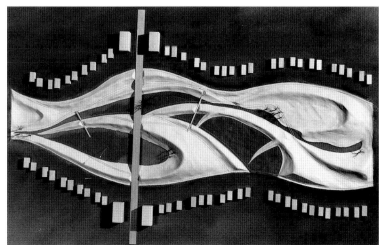

Lee Cott

Design Critic in Urban Planning and Design

Mark Johnson

Visiting Design Critic in Landscape Architecture

Since 1989, Denver's civic leaders, real estate developers, open space advocates, and community activists have worked diligently to begin redeveloping the old Stapleton Airport. Closed for two and a half years—4700 acres in size with 145 buildings, 1000 acres of concrete paving, and numerous environmental issues— this problem has vexed planning and implementation efforts. With an approved, highly acclaimed plan in place, the project remains dormant for one vital reason: difficulty in setting priorities and determining the critical framework elements that the project must meet in order to be built.

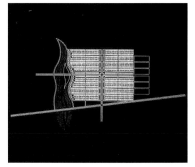

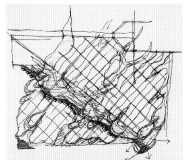

Key to the framework is the need for a design vision that possesses both the framework and the design detail to demonstrate how open space and community should be integrated in a functional, market-driven plan that integrates all elements of the remolded city into a sustainable whole. The studio asked the question, "How can community development patterns and open spaces combine to reclaim the site as a healthy urban growth center?" With several years of professional planning in place, students were asked to challenge traditional thinking to demonstrate the clearest vision of what this place should become. The study area encompassed roughly 2000 acres of the urban infill site surrounded by existing residential and industrial neighborhoods.

The Stapleton Project is at a critical point at this time. This studio had the ability to play a key role in triggering important decisions that are urgently needed to catalyze redevelopment with the best possible thinking.

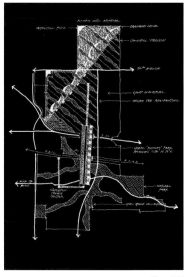

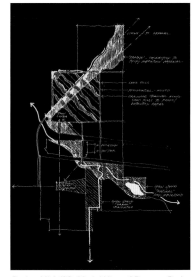

Landscape architecture, urban planning and design, and architecture students were needed to meet the challenge of developing interdisciplinary design solutions. Students worked alone except during the analysis phase.

Terrall Vern Budge MLA '99, Model View of Runway Park, Model View of Prairie Landform, and Study Diagrams

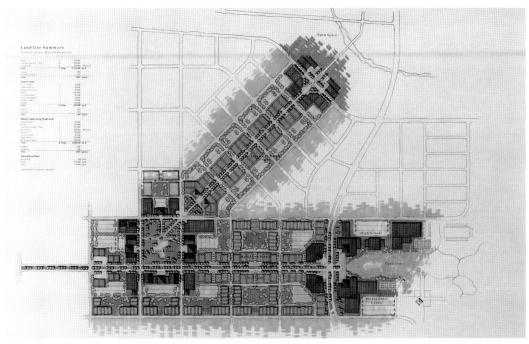

Fran Reiner MLA '98, Town Center/Detail District Plan

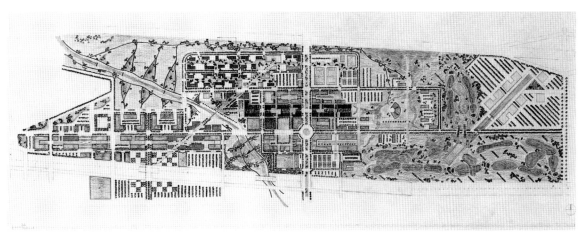

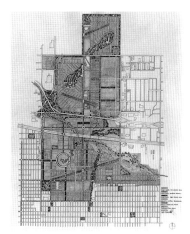

Tetsuya Fujie MLA '98, Stapleton Airport Development Plans

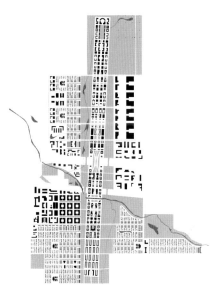

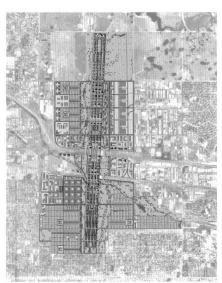

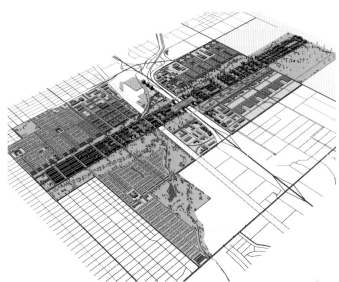

Thomas Hester MAUD '98 and Kimberly Everett MUP '98, Stapleton Airport Masterplan: Figure/Ground, Masterplan with Surrounding Context, and Masterplan with Recommended Buildout

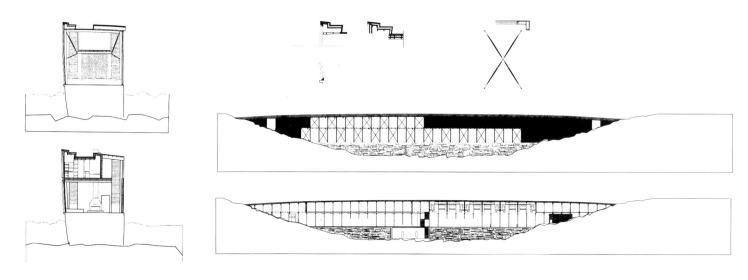

North Sea Field Research Laboratory

Jan Olav Jensen
Kenzo Tange Visiting Design Critic in Architecture

A continued and accelerating physical "colonization" of the surface of the earth by humankind may give the impression that architects only have to deal with urban situations in manmade contexts. This is certainly true in most cases today. But this impression, if not corrected, may also limit the vocabulary of the architect, because fundamental architectural issues may simply be overlooked or never addressed.

The choice of project for this studio was based on the belief that an awareness of the fundamental architectural problems that arise in their purest form when dealing with environments untouched by man, may prove a strength in future situations and ideally will give the architect an even stronger awareness of what culture means. The choice of project was also based on a belief that the period of study is a most precious time. It is the period when the architect has the possibility to get to know his or her personal talents, abilities, and potential. I believe that being unaware of one's own affinities or powers eliminates one of the main driving forces when practicing architecture, thus making the architect an unconscious subscriber to any number of popular movements. An effective way of increasing the awareness of one's architectural goals is to set up "laboratory-like" architectural experiments and closely watch the emerging results. This project was one such experiment, though with an absolutely pragmatic and realistic location and brief.

The studio investigated a rather small but complex program of a research laboratory of about 2000 square meters, located on Selsholmen Island, on the Norwegian coast. The location of the building, on a remote island far out in the sea, is important in giving instant and continuous access to the project's main areas of interest.

The functions of the research laboratory are twofold: 1) continuous surveillance of the North Sea, and 2) provision of time-limited specific research projects that need a field base. Since the island is a desert island, all necessary programmatic elements must be specially created—port facilities, housing for researchers, infrastructure such as roads, and so on. Students could establish the program as one building or as several smaller units that are located close or far away from each other.

An important issue was how architecture is established on a site that does not have any trace of human activity, and that does not give explicit manmade clues to the architect. The additions and/or subtractions of the architect, in such a place, are certainly based upon a set of references, but these references or clues are put to a test as they are not physically present, but rather the mental "luggage" of the architect.

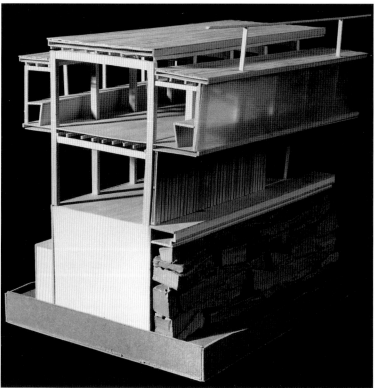

Annegret Schaible MArch '99, Elevations, Sections, and Plans, and Model Views

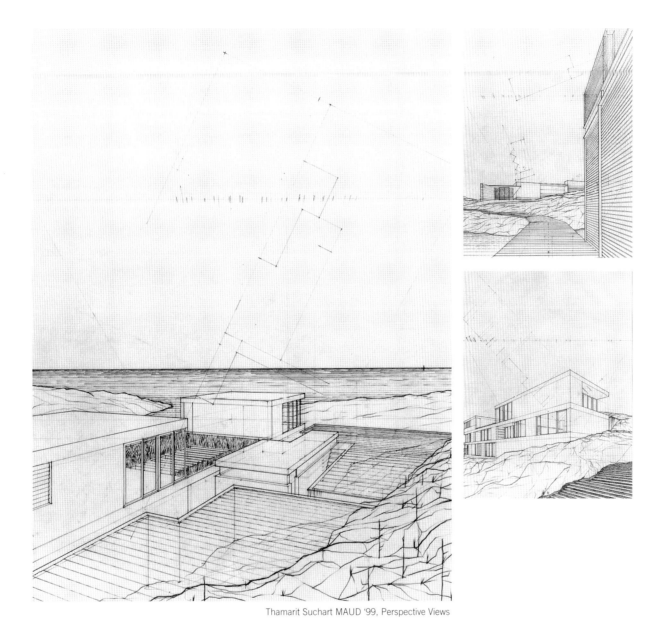

Thamarit Suchart MAUD '99, Perspective Views

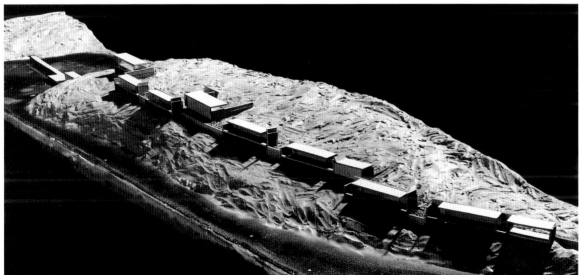

Monica Rivera MArch '99, Model View and Perspective Views

Between the Lines: The Performative Surface, Public Life, and the Architecture of Entertainment

Sheila Kennedy

Associate Professor of Architecture

This studio used the design of a contemporary cineplex in Boston's downtown theater district as a vehicle to explore how the radiant infrastructure of electrical illumination, information communication, and heating and cooling can become inextricably intertwined with architecture. As much a speculative and critical projection of the imagination as a technical project, the studio investigated design strategies that reclaim the substantial service territories (up to 35% of the building volume of the cineplex), and the formal possibilities of infrastructure as a third term between public and private capable of mediating between the interior space needs of the program and the public life of the city.

The studio focused on the spatial implications of radiance, as both a specific physical property of materials and as a contemporary architectural condition of intense internal presence. Students in the studio examined these phenomena as both an extension and critique of ideas of "depth," "poché," and modern notions of transparency, lightweight construction, and skin. The radiant infrastructures of the cineplex produce effects of artificial light and color, media and heat that can be liberated from their distributory body/containers to participate with architecture to create space. The architectural consequences of this emancipation were explored as students developed speculative new programs for the seemingly banal building surfaces of partition, curtain wall, chase space, suspended floor, and hung ceiling that characterize the contemporary cineplex typology. Students considered what it means to conceive of these floor, ceiling, and wall assemblies as performative surfaces that join the formerly distinct categories of furniture, architecture, and infrastructure, and offer the potential to rethink the form, public presence, and programmatic organization of the architecture of entertainment.

Through analysis of modern cinema precedents and contemporary techniques of cinematography and photographic imaging, students developed selected building components in creating large-scale models and drawings. An important part of this process was the discovery of what may be termed a "catachrestic" use of post-industrial standardized materials. This involves a careful inventory of the specific physical properties of the material, combined with an amnesia toward the standardized applications of the product, and a willingness to invent new uses for the material that are both a "misuse" of the material and a demonstration of its fullest use.

This studio was sponsored by Runtal North America, Inc., an international manufacturer of radiant heating infrastructures. Students worked in collaboration with mechanical engineers who made presentations and offered technical support for the students' projects. Marco Steinberg was the teaching assistant for the studio.

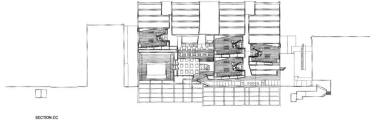

SECTION CC

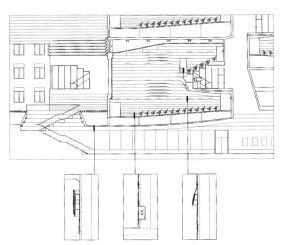

Matthew LaRue MArch '99, Model View and Sections

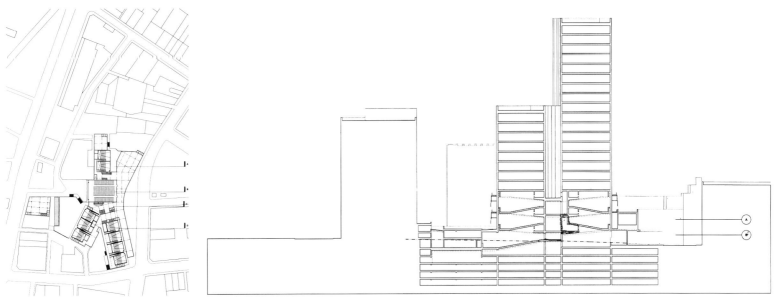

Gullivar Shepard MArch '99, Plan and Section

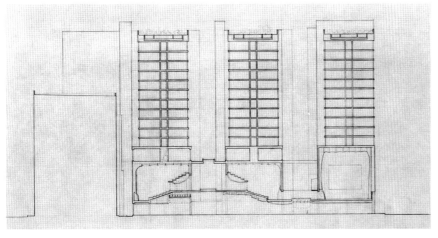

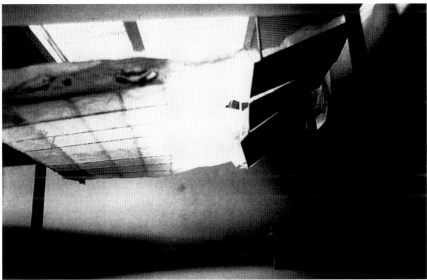

Erica Sangster MArch '99, Section and Model Views

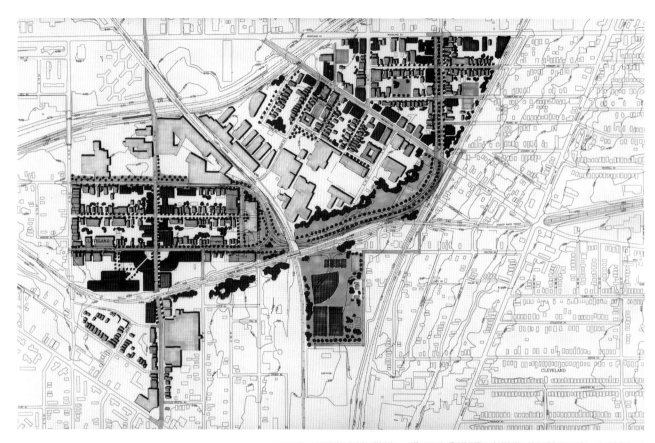

Designing The Urban Parkway as a Catalyst for Redevelopment

David Lee
Adjunct Professor of Urban Planning and Design

In 1950, the City of Cleveland was the fifth largest city in the country and along with Pittsburgh, Detroit, and Chicago, the industrial heart of the nation. Like many American cities, however, Cleveland proper has seen a steady decline in population and loss of jobs as the suburbs have grown in population. In recent years, jobs in industry and manufacturing have increasingly moved to areas outside the city.

Today, however, Cleveland is experiencing a resurgence with the highly publicized Rock and Roll Hall of Fame, new basketball and baseball stadiums downtown, and new residential and commercial activity.

A task force of public and private sector representatives has identified a series of core transportation projects that might stimulate economic development activity. A new parkway linking an existing interstate highway interchange with a university research center and passing through a variety of neighborhoods, including residential areas and underutilized heavy industries is proposed.

This studio focused on the design of the parkway and the reconfiguration of the areas through which it passes in order to enhance existing assets and generate creative options for new development and the adaptive reuse of existing resources.

This design-oriented studio explored large-scale urban design and landscape issues, and proposed specific architectural interventions as well. The group was interdisciplinary and worked in teams as well as individually. There were two trips to Cleveland paid for by the sponsor of the studio, University Circle Inc.

The issues that were addressed by the studio included general planning policy and market feasibility, streetscape and open space design, transit integration, and conceptual architectural design.

Nadir Ait-Laoussine MLA/MUP '99, Justin Grigg MLA '98, and Ela Seraroglu MUP '99, Master Plan and Illustrative Site Plan

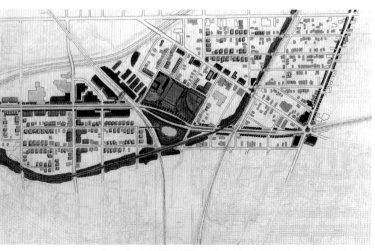

Caren Garfield MUP '99 and Ryan Tam MUP '98, Illustrative Site Plan

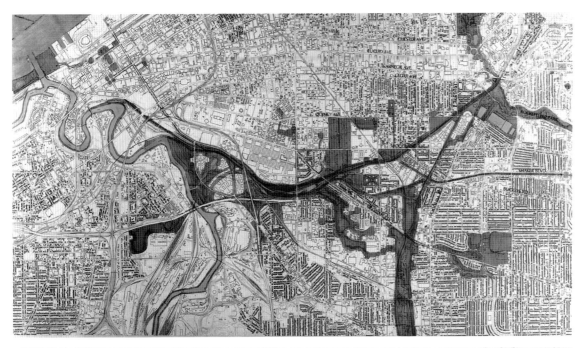

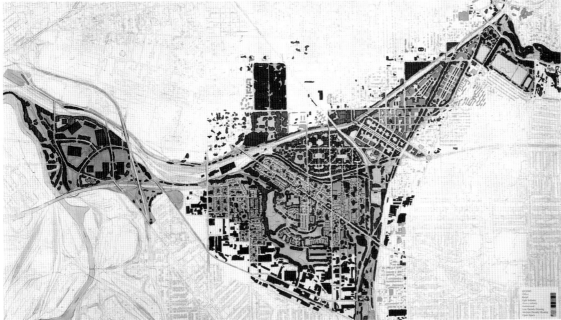

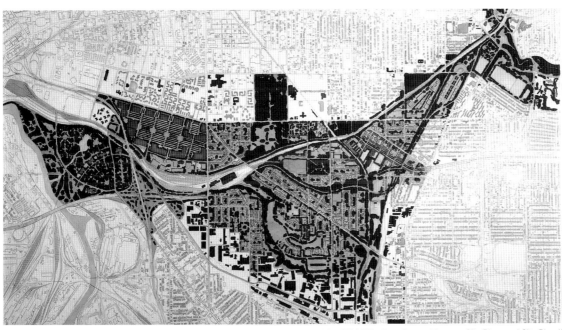

Heather Culp MUP '99, Amy Cupples-Rubiano MLA '98, and David Robbins MLA '98, Open Space Diagram, Site Plan, and Site Plan II

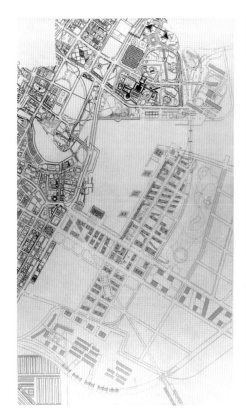

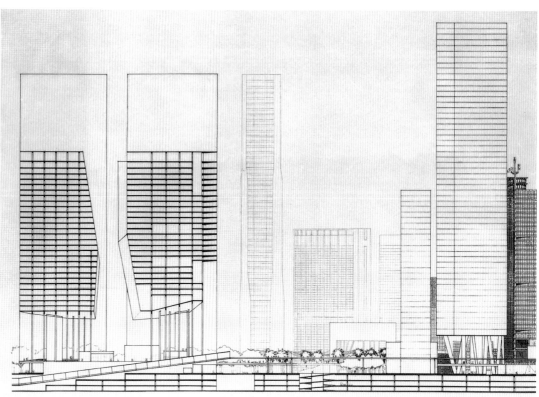

New Urbanity: The Case of Marina Bay, Singapore

Rodolfo Machado
Professor in Practice of Architecture and Urban Design

This was the third and last studio dedicated to the investigation and design of new urban conditions for Singapore's Central District. This trilogy was sponsored by the Urban Redevelopment Authority (URA), for which we are grateful. The site is the largest urban piece generated by recent water reclamation projects. The program contains office space and residential quarters, plus the myriad of programmatic elements that are essential for the production of a sense of urbanity.

The studio required a site visit, which took place during the spring break; the midterm review was held in Singapore in the office of the URA.

Gad Liwerant MArch '98 and Pablo Savid-Buteler MArch '99,
Site Plan, Section, Perspective Views, and Axonometric View

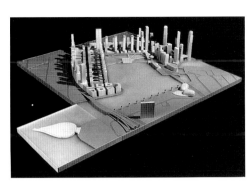

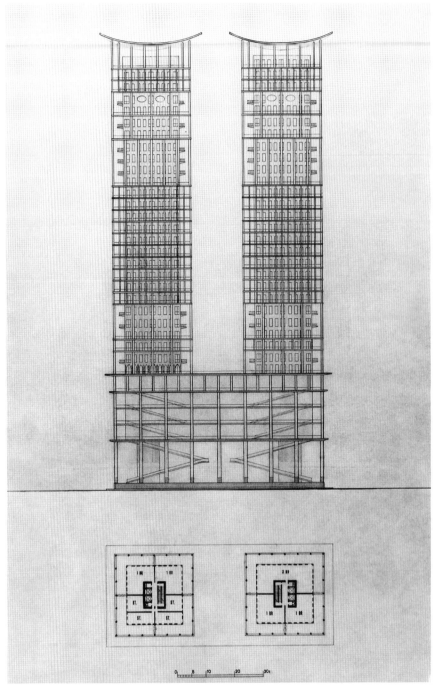

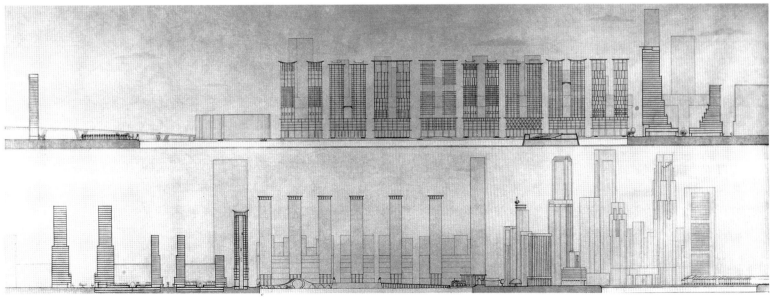

Claudia Bancalari MArch '99 and Kevin Storm MAUD '99, Model View, Perspective Views, Veranda Tower: Plan and Elevation, and Marina Bay Section/Elevation

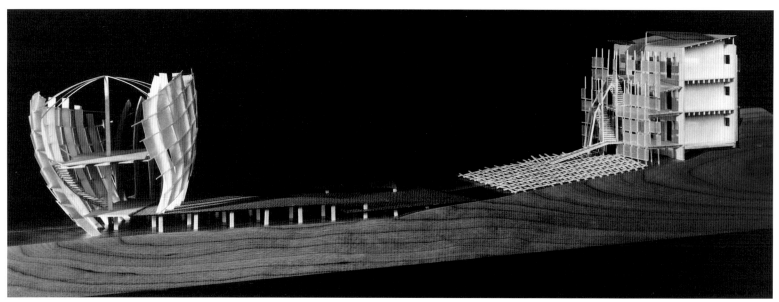

Michael Gale MArch '99, Model View

Empathy and Abstraction: Craft, Site and the Virtual

Malcolm McCullough
Associate Professor of Architecture

Charles Rose
Visiting Design Critic in Architecture

Maryann Thompson
Visiting Design Critic in Architecture

This studio emphasized site architecture and material expression, especially in relation to the virtual. Working with a powerful, difficult site divided by a large piece of environmental infrastructure, and with a proven small program based on month-long internships in a site-sensitized setting, the studio developed projects for an Arts Center at the river outlet hurricane storm surge barrier in Providence, Rhode Island.

As site architecture, projects worked from the ground up—in this case from the constructed ground of an infilled urban waterfront. Conceptually, such work aimed to overcome tendencies to design sites around preconceived buildings, that is, to "put" figurative buildings on neutral grounds. By contrast, the elements and strategies of site design, and of heavy waterfront construction in particular, became the basis for the architecture.

With regard to materiality, projects attempted to go beyond the diagram toward a more tectonic expression, and to do so with the benefit of textural and lighting studies in digital media. Here, the attempt to overcome a usual tendency was directed toward issues of the substance and orientation in new media: we wished, in digital models, for there to be more of a there, there. And regardless of medium, we wished to attain the kind of resolution that a smaller (30,000 sq. ft.) building can allow in a semester timeframe.

And concerning the virtual, we simply wished to point out that we live and practice in an age where more and more people, even architects at times, mistake the representation for the reality. We want to be on the lookout for people forgetting the masses, microclimates, geographies, and orientational aspects of sited reality, as well as the appropriable and enduring aspects of non-trademarked place. We believe that it has become a part of design education to understand and counter the possibility of spatial "de-skilling."

Ann Bergren MArch '99, Perspective Views

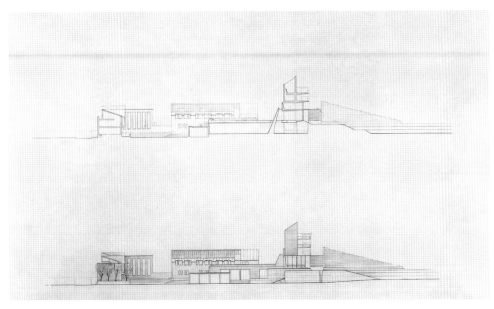

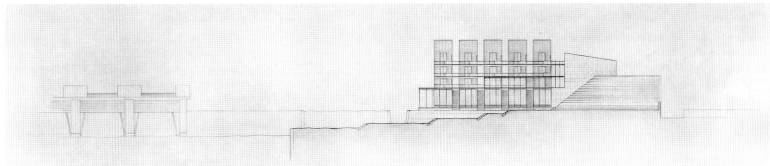

Guillemette deBoucaud MArch '99, Sections and Elevations

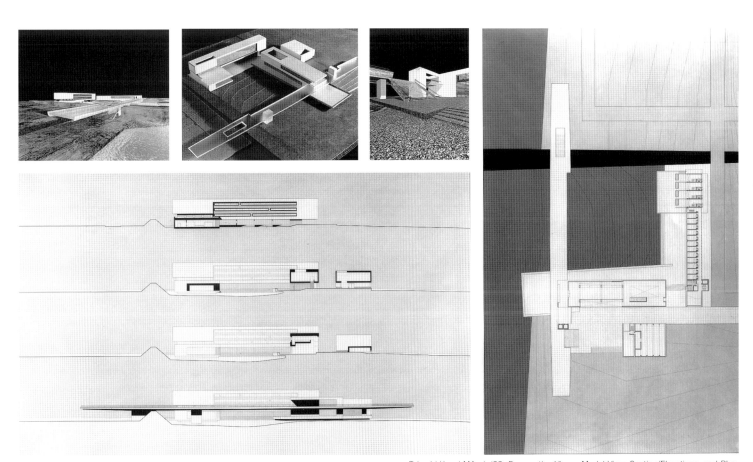

Takashi Yanai MArch '99, Perspective Views, Model View, Section/Elevations, and Plan

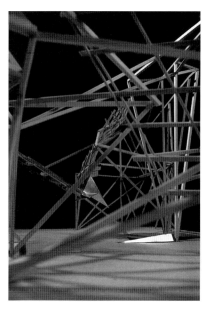

Marshall Brown MArch '99, Model Views

The Other J.L. Sert

Enric Miralles
Design Critic in Architecture

Again

"Do it Again…"

To establish a critical distance with the recent past…and, at the same time, to learn from specific buildings within concrete places.

Start to work the project like a dialogue—guided by curiosity and desire to learn…

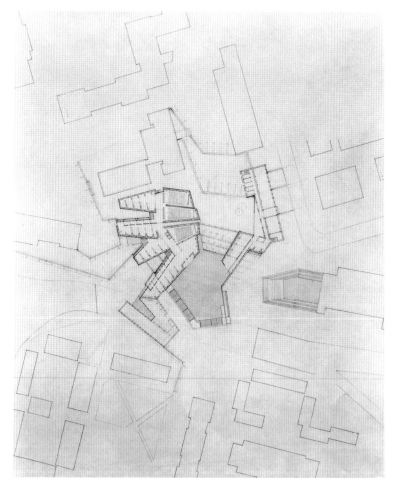

The studio projects I offered in previous semesters ("A Double Please" and "The Other Quincy Street") were exercises on contemplation and conservation…

The idea of place change, "A Double Please," was a moment in time—an American building from the 1970s; "The Other Quincy Street" was a street…an everyday street.

Now, the place is the Architect himself—Josep Lluis Sert. Inside the architect…the ambitions, etc.; a personal experience explored with reference to specific places.

The buildings in the vicinity of the GSD were our main subject. (Some jumps into later buildings at Barcelona and Mallorca were allowed). This was accomplished in two ways: first, by seeing the physical reality of a place through the random position of some commissions, and later, through repeating these experiences inside our class…

Each J.L. Sert building was done again.

In the end, I think J.L. Sert was an elegant conversationalist (and conversation at that).

The buildings we took as our point of departure were:
Center for the Study of World Religion, J.L. Sert, 1959
Holyoke Center, J.L. Sert, 1962
Peabody Terrace, J.L. Sert, 1963-64
Undergraduate Science Center, J.L. Sert, 1966-68

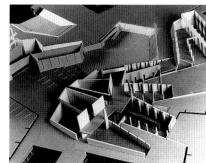

Michelle J. Kim MArch '99, Plan and Model View

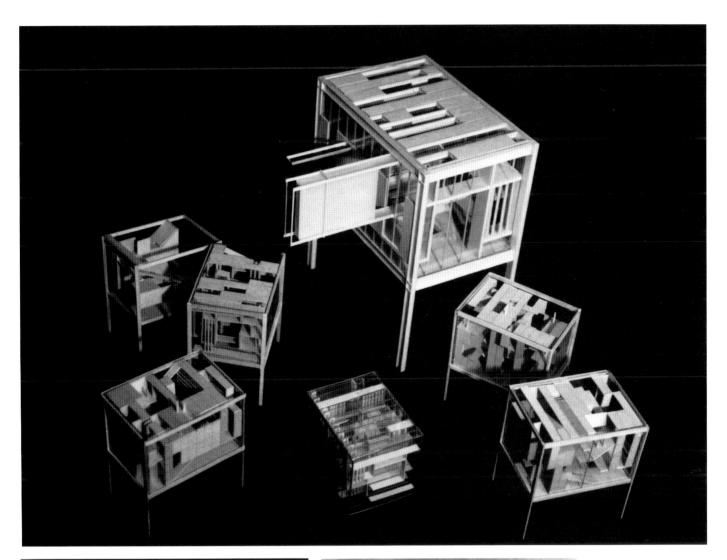

Gustavo Arango MAUD '98, Model Views of Recreational Cells, Photomontage: Movie Theater, and Photomontage: Crew Museum

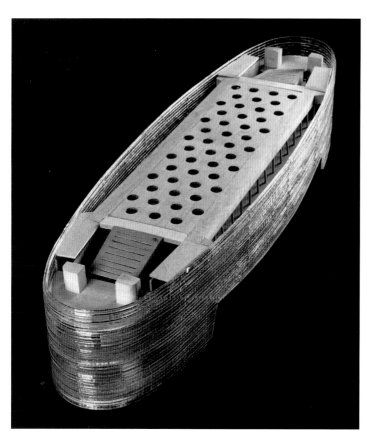

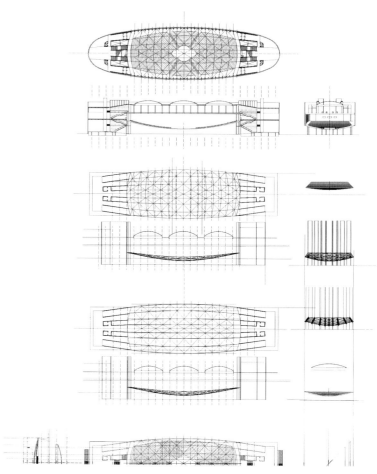

Timothy Dumbleton MArch '99, Model View and Analytic Drawing

The End of the Building Design Process

Rafael Moneo

Josep Lluis Sert Professor of Architecture

This studio focused on the last steps of the design process. We are accustomed to working by proceeding from an architecturally abstract definition that directly suggests a structural solution. It seems this salient structure finally prevails and it becomes the dominant way of thinking about architecture after Modernism. And yet, with the perspective of a practicing professional, one realizes how much the finishing of buildings requires of an architect. In "dressing" the naked structure of the building, one confronts many problems, among them the very important issue of the definition of indoor and outdoor.

The studio took an undeveloped building: Louis Kahn's beautiful proposal for a Congress Hall for Venice, Italy. I hoped that the students would not be intimidated by assuming the work of such a gifted architect. The project could be understood as a valuable tool to help us advance the definitive aspects of a building. We were not looking for the missing Kahn building. Given the structure of his proposal, we proceeded to define the architecture of a final design for another building. We experienced precisely how much buildings lack definition until they are designed with respect to entrances, doors, walls, ceilings, lights, appliances, colors, etc. Precision in design is an essential characteristic of all architecture.

Through this process we saw how open to definition architecture remains in spite of the structural strength of the existing proposal. The studio helped us understand which features of a building define its architecture. The different scale of these features had to be carefully understood in order to combine them in a final architectural proposal. This experience had remarkable results considering the value of the structure from which we started, and the requirements of the program.

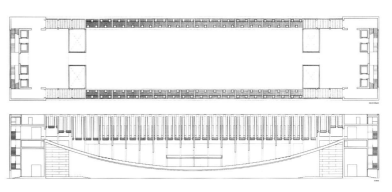

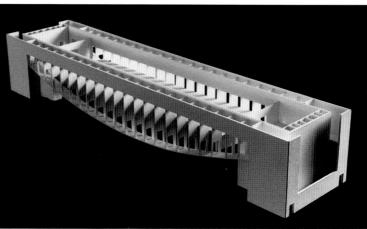

Lindsay Smith MArch '99, Plan, Longitudinal Section, and Model View

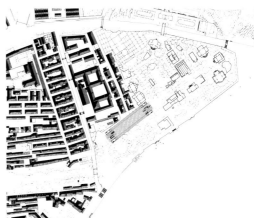

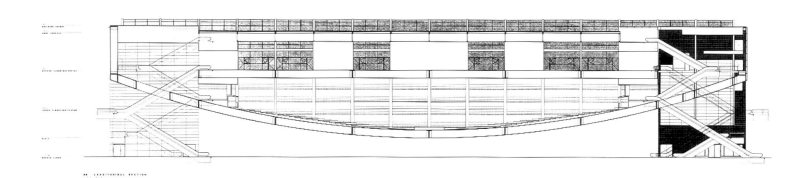

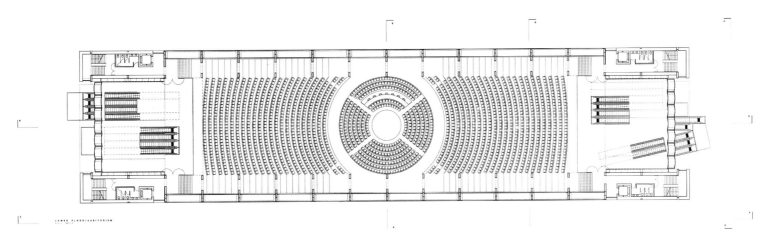

Ho San Chang MArch '99, Model View, Site Plan, Longitudinal Section, and Plan

Everyday Extra-Ordinary: Urban and Domestic Inhabitation in New York City Through Exploration of Materials

Toshiko Mori
Professor in Practice of Architecture

This studio focused its premise on an exploration of the elements and constructs that constitute daily and routine situations of everyday life. The specific method of exploration was through materiality, fabrication, and the detailing of artifacts. The site was New York City.

As a resident in a city, one's domestic private and internal life intersects constantly with urban, public, and external circumstances. If one of the most optimistic aims of architecture is to improve the quality of life, everyday routine circumstances become highly influential in our lives because of the sheer quantity of repetition and cumulative effect. They are often ignored since they are not conscious acts that modify the course of our lives. Yet they constitute a significant part of the ritual fabric of our lives and, without them, one loses the sense of engagement to a specific environment.

Tactility was introduced as the starting point of the studio: tactility as the physical sensation of touch, the mental information of the texture of the spaces, and the complex series of socio-cultural references evoked by characterizing and identifying the artifacts. Tactility is both personal and universal, intimate and distant, literal and figurative. Therefore "tangible" and "intangible," or "material" and "immaterial," or "visible" and "invisible" issues may exist parallel to each other.

In order to start the project, we visited a Laboratory of Materials in New York City called Materials ConneZions that houses recently developed materials to study and research the property, history, fabrication process, and application possibilities. Each student selected one material as a principal resource for research and development.

The first phase of the studio involved design of the following urban artifacts, and testing the results of research on materials: a phone booth in the West Village, a newsstand in Union Square, and a bus stop in Soho. The second phase of the semester was devoted to the design of domestic artifacts and inhabitation in New York City.

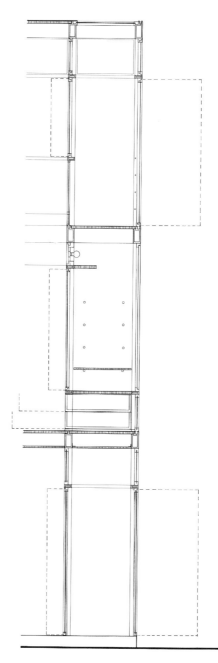

Delphine Yip MArch '99, Model View, Photomontage of
Proposed Building on Site, Wall Section

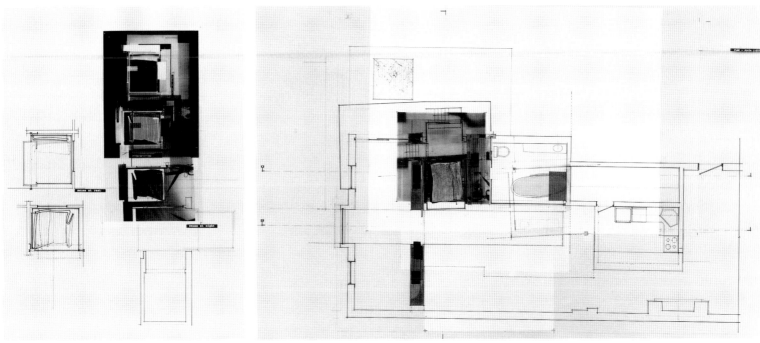

Amale Andraos MArch '99, Section Transformations and Plan of Sauna

Maiya K. Dos MArch '99, Perspective Views showing Light and Reflection Conditions

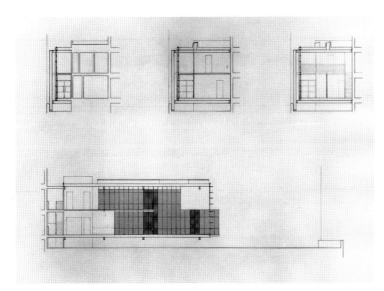

Tamara Metz MArch '99, Section and Model View

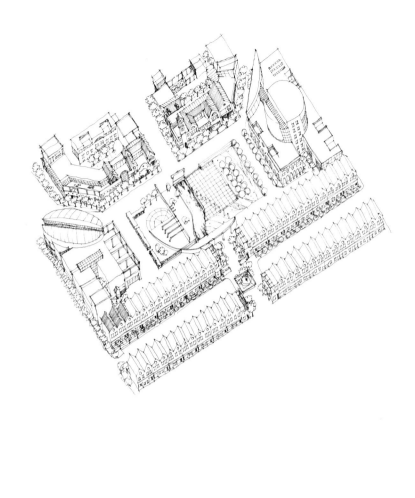

A Place for All...Development Strategies for the Virginia Beach Resort Area

Martha O'Mara
*Assistant Professor of Real Estate Development
in the Fields of Management and Organizational Behavior*

Scott Levitan
Visiting Design Critic in Urban Planning and Design

Virginia Beach is the summer playground for the Chesapeake Bay region, and is also Virginia's most populous year-round city. Developed at the end of the rail spur from Norfolk, the high-energy oceanfront precipitously trails off into a late-20th-century suburban settlement. Without a historic core to provide ballast, the challenge facing the community is to retrace its steps and organize itself physically and to accept its role as the center of a metropolitan region of 2,000,000 people. The studio evaluated the factors guiding planning and envisioned opportunities for grounding the city as an all-weather home to accommodate its regional place. The studio was sponsored by the City of Virginia Beach and included a trip to this 'accidental city' hosted by Mayor Meyera Oberndorf. Students worked in small interdisciplinary teams of students from all degree programs. Learning goals included demographic research analysis, urban planning and design, and real estate development modeling skills. Each team produced an urban design concept for a particular site within the Virginia Beach Resort Area study district and supported their design concept with market and financial feasibility reports.

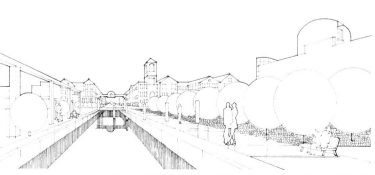

Erika Oliver MUP '99, Nina Tam MDesS '98, and Bing Wang MAUD '99, Axonometric View of Mixed Use Development and Perspective Views

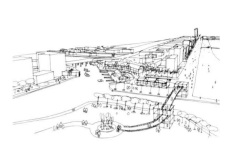

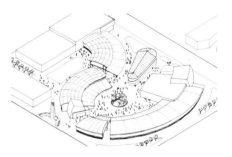

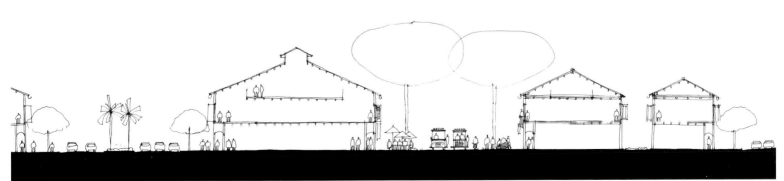

Bernard Chan MAUD '99, Jeong-Ah Choi MUP '99, and Mauricio Silva MDesS '98, Perspective Views, Site Plan, and Section

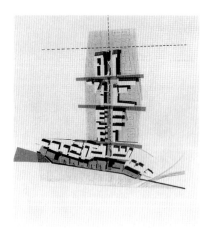
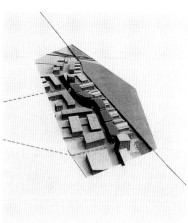

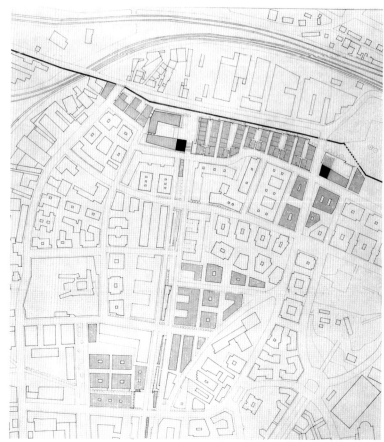

Attraversare la Città: Redevelopment around the Via Appia Nuova in Rome

Peter Rowe

Raymond Garbe Professor of Architecture and Urban Design

Hashim Sarkis

Assistant Professor of Architecture

As cultural artifacts, cities embody many of our aims and aspirations with regard to day-to-day life, help guide many of our civilizing tendencies, provide the backdrop for many of our extraordinary celebrations, and encapsulate much of our history. They are determined by what we ask of them as well as in turn determining of our own lives within them. They change over time as we change, while also serving as change agents and marking both events by their very existence and continuing evolution. Over time, memories fade, past events are forgotten and the parts of a city that once played host to those experiences take on altered meanings, new associations, and support different livelihoods.

The area along and in the vicinity of the Via Appia Nuova in Rome—stretching from San Giovanni in Laterano, inside the old wall, to Parco Santo Stefano well outside the wall in the southeast—is an urban quarter embodying many of these characteristics. Some parts are old and some are new. Indeed, areas along the Via Appia Nuova and several of its major cross-streets and intersections represent a veritable transect through Roman urban history, especially since the turn of the century, and a rich reservoir of specific urban experiences. It remains, nevertheless, an under-recognized and poorly understood section of the city, especially in comparison to many other areas.

The aim of the studio was twofold. The first was to demonstrate how a substantial urban area in Rome might acquire a greater sense of local identity, recover both greater day-to-day life and contact with its own history, and develop a broader range of viable public open spaces and operative cultural venues. The second was to propose specific redevelopment projects for the area, addressing issues such as improved circulation and access, economic revitalization, improved visibility of major historic and recreation areas, and greater general coordination among potential infrastructure improvements and adjacent building projects and land uses.

The studio was sponsored and performed in collaboration with ACER (Associazione Costruttori Edili di Roma) and INArch (Istituto Nazionale Architettura). A site visit was made to Rome during the spring break and special assistance was provided throughout the term by Professor Rosario Pavia from Rome.

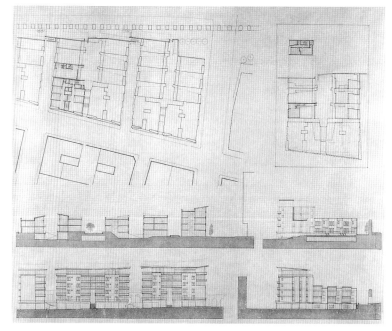

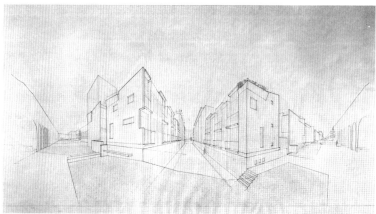

Beverly Choe MAUD '99, Axis Diagram, Street Wall Diagram, Site Plan, Housing Plan, Sections, Elevations, and Perspective View of Housing

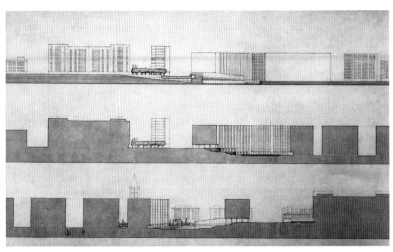

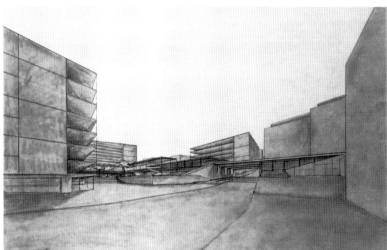

James Gresalfi MAUD '99 and Gregory J. Haley MAUD '98, Sections, Perspective View, and Model View of Master Plan along Rail Corridor

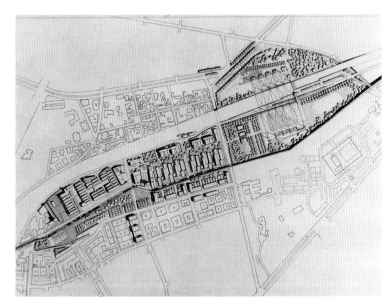

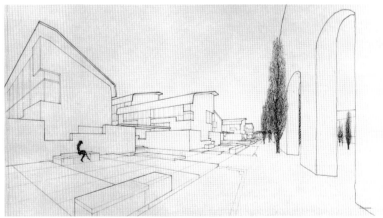

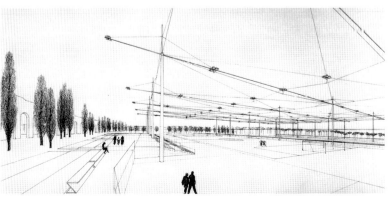

Martin Zogran MAUD '99, Felice Aquaduct Development Plan, Perspective View of Aquaduct Housing, and Perspective View of Urban Sky Structure

Doing and Dancing: Rudolf Laban and the "Dance Farm"

Mack Scogin
Kajima Adjunct Professor of Architecture

In 1910 Rudolf Laban founded, for lack of a better term, a "dance farm" at Lago Verbano (Lago Maggiore), Switzerland. At the "dance farm," the whole community, after work, produced dances based on their occupational experiences. The "dance farm" idea came from Laban's desire to lead people back to a life in which art grows from their experiences. Laban believed, the "aim of man was his festive existence, not the way of gluttony and uselessness, but as a means of developing his personality, as a chance to lift him into those spheres of life which distinguished man from animal." Through this experience of the "dance farm" Laban realized more and more that his "dramas, songs and movement-scenes, in spite of the occasional use of the spoken word, did not belong to drama or opera but to the world of dance."

It can be argued that dance, more than any other art form, most closely resembles the fundamental characteristics of architecture. As in architecture, it:

1. Traces space, time, and movement, relies on light, content, context, structure, and timing for order.
2. Is constructed of the human figure and occupied by the human spirit.
3. Involves a relentless struggle with the natural forces of gravity and the individual limitations of human physicality.
4. Employs the illusionary effects of procession, perspective, point-of-view, color, and light.
5. Demands precise technique and craft.
6. Requires knowledge of its traditions, history, and theory for substance and orientation.
7. Stimulates an awareness of the reciprocal line between the body and mind.

More importantly, like architecture, dance as movement is a central feature of human existence, a medium through which inner attitudes are displaced, learning is achieved and by which experience is enlarged. Both dance and architecture are performances.

This studio's aim was to look to the subject of dance to inform an architecture that embodies the individual student's developed principles of a late-twentieth-century performance.

The more specific context of the study was defined by three basic considerations:

1. The beliefs, theories and practices of Rudolf Laban, seen by many to be the creator and founder of the modern art of dance.
2. A program for a dance center to include space for instruction, performance, physical therapy, and community activity.
3. A site on Fort Point Channel in Boston between the New Federal Court House and the Boston Children's Museum.

Luis Eduardo Boza MArch '99, Model View and Conceptual Perspective

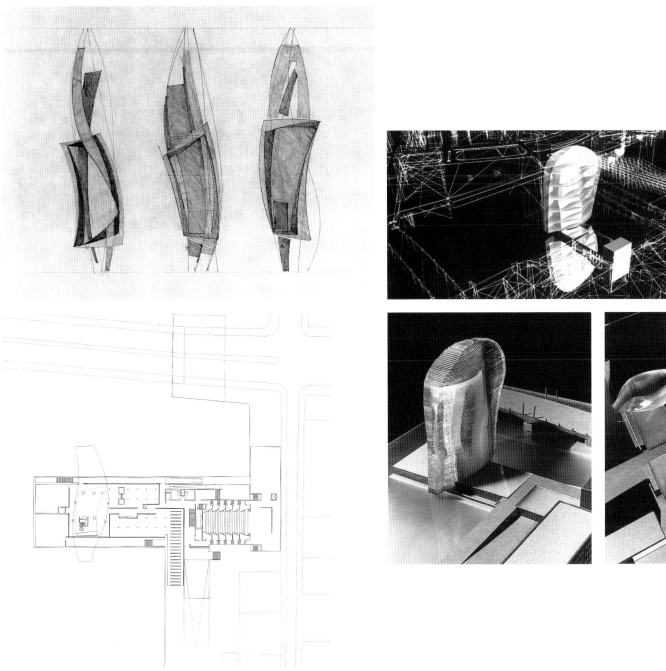

Shane Williamson MArch '99, Conceptual Plans, Plan, Aerial View, and Model Views

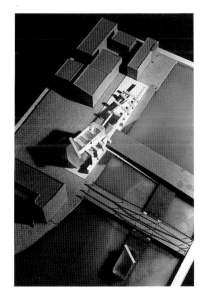

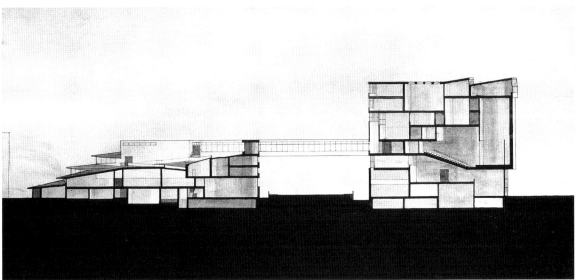

Jennifer Neuwalder MArch '99, Model View and Section

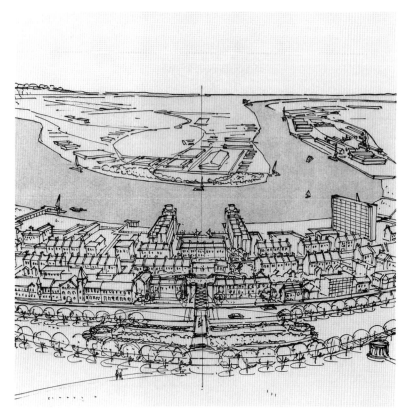

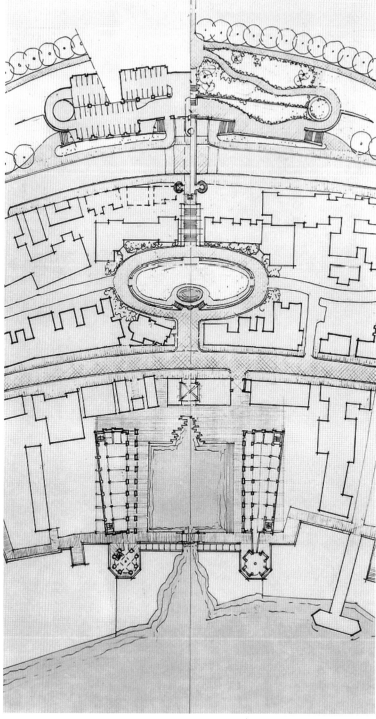

New Urban Strategies for the Historic Waterfront of Rochester and Chatham, England

Barry Shaw
Visiting Design Critic in Urban Planning and Design

Waterfront revitalization has been a key element in the redevelopment of many small cities during the last two decades. Containerization, changing patterns of trace, and the peace dividend have meant that working waterfronts have largely disappeared. Cities, which previously turned their backs on the water, are now presented with an opportunity to revitalize their environments and economies. There is a great deal of experience in North America and Europe which allows for a critical discussion of waterfront regeneration strategies.

The studio concentrated on the towns of Rochester and Chatham, which have developed along the river Medway in Kent. The closure of the historic dock-yard in Chatham, as well as most of the waterfront-related industries along major stretches of the riverside in the heart of the urban area, have damaged the local economy and created vacant and underused sites. A changing regional economy responding to the opportunities presented by the Channel Tunnel and the government regeneration initiative, called Thames Gateway, will require new infrastructure and new housing. Recent waterfront developments in London and Cardiff, as well as Boston, Lowell, Salem, and Mystic Seaport, were taken as reference models to support discussion of new regeneration strategies in historic areas.

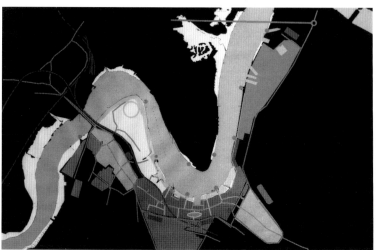

Steve Scapicchio MAUD '99, Bird's Eye Perspective,
Site Plan, and Transportation Modification Diagram

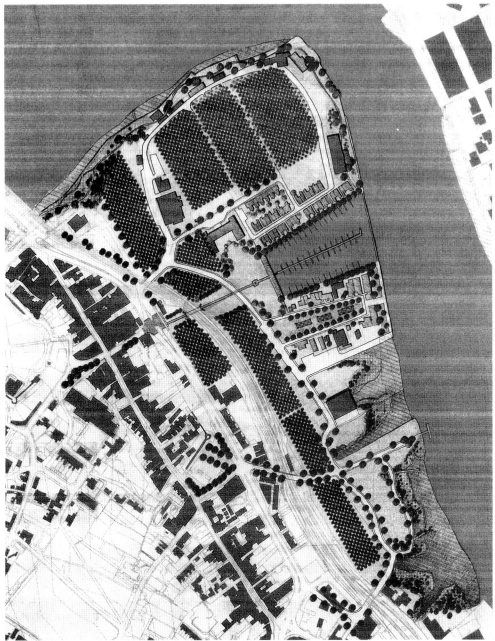

Ann Parker MAUD '99, Plan of Phase One: Planting and Phytoremediation

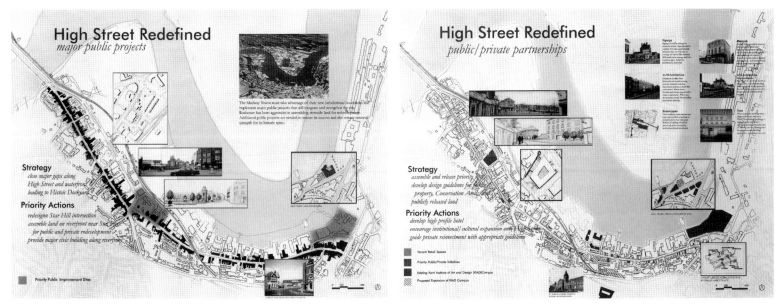

Eric E. Dray MAUD '99, High Street Redefined: Major Public Projects and High Street Redefined: Public/Private Partnerships

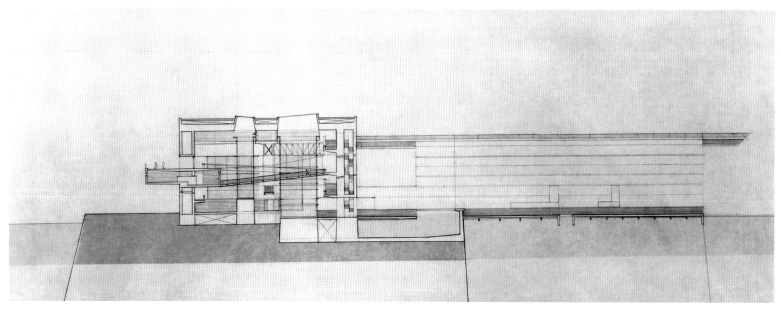

A Project Along the River Bilbao

Jorge Silvetti
Nelson Robinson, Jr., Professor of Architecture

Francisco Mangado
Visiting Design Critic in Architecture

During the last two decades, the Basque city of Bilbao and its surroundings have been the object of very important urban and infrastructural transformations, resulting from intensive industrialization and the economic changes this brought with it. The swift urbanization created major changes in the landscape along the river, whose character came to be defined by the presence of factory buildings and as well as housing for immigrant workers. With Spain's economic crisis in the 1970s, many of the factories were closed and subsequently demolished. While it was necessary to provide new alternatives both in terms of employment and housing to the area's inhabitants, the city was also obligated to develop new activities as well as to investigate new urban and territorial models for metropolitan Bilbao. The areas of particular focus were the zones along the riverbanks.

In the 1990s, various public administrations involved in the problem commissioned architectural projects that provide the city with new services and a new identity as a vital center of the Basque region. Some of them, like Frank Gehry's Guggenheim Museum, have become a symbol for the city. Other projects that are less well-known but just as important, include Norman Foster's new subway system as well as several new bridges and a new airport by Santiago Calatrava.

From the analysis of some specific architectonic programs fixed according to the conclusions of the urban studies of the fall semester studio, also sited in Bilbao, conducted by Jorge Silvetti and Rodolfo Machado, this studio addressed the question of the capacity of the architecture itself to both transform the physical context and generate expectations capable of regenerating the entire area of analysis. The studio focused on two specific instances: the proposed new "Athletics" soccer stadium in the Deusto area of the City of Bilbao and the proposed public aquarium in the Barakaldo area. Each student developed only one of these projects. The sponsor of this studio, which is part of an ongoing research project, was the Diputacion Foral de Bizkaia (the highest regional authority).

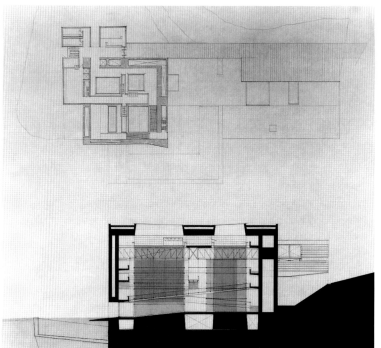

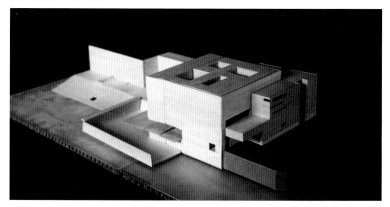

Gabriela Bojalil MArch '98, Section, Plan and Section, and Model View

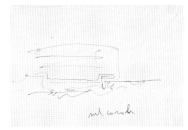

Matteo Scagnol MArch '99, Site Plan, Model Views, and Project Sketch

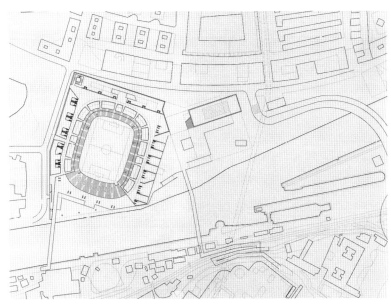
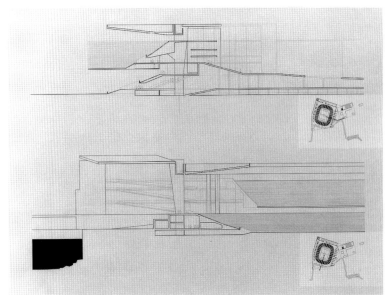
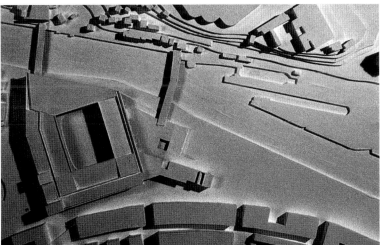

Victor Sant'Anna MAUD '99, Site Plan, Model View, and Longitudinal Sections

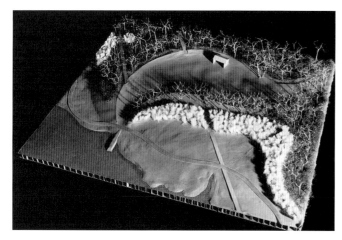

Eric F. Kramer MLA '98, Model View, Perspective View, and Site Plan of Proposed Intervention

Learning from Nature

Jacques Simon

Visiting Design Critic in Landscape Architecture

Our intent is to train landscape architects to become accustomed to dealing with complexity, so that they can distinguish between what is truly significant and what is secondary. However, this approach should not prevent the student who is focusing on his/her project from taking side roads: it gives an opportunity to consider the same project from different points of view.

A group of students can work on the same site, each student trying to solve a different problem, so that they realize that they are not working on an autonomous project; they are participating in a common reflection. Knowing that every project, even a modest one, implies dealing with goals that often surpass students' abilities, it would be interesting to develop an interactive approach.

The objective of the studio was to develop a project that consisted of defining a territory, and more specifically, an urban one with all its components. We chose a significant example in order to put into practice a methodology that enabled us to draw up an inventory of all components of the territory, and to study and analyze what is specific to this place. Then, we suggested a picture of the place, as well as a particular vocabulary, referring to the vegetation, the equipment, the colors...

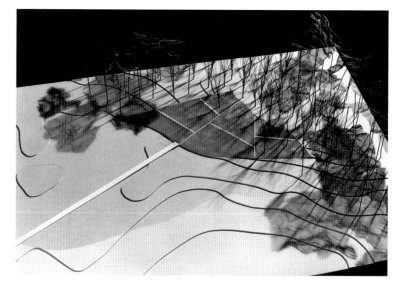

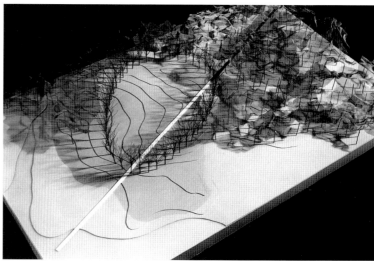

Claudia Taborda MLA '99, Conceptual Model: Look Out and
Conceptual Model: Outside-Upland-Marsh

Vardit Tsurnamal MLA '99, Site Plan and Perspective Views

Misty March MLA '99, Photomontages: Stone Filter, Log Filter, Hedge Filter, and Swale Filter

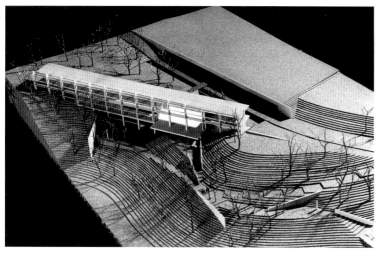

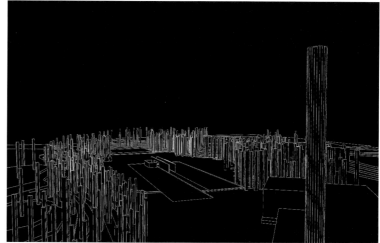

Robin Sakahara MLA '98, Model View

The Nasher Collection Garden at Wellesley College

Michael Van Valkenburgh

Charles Eliot Professor in Practice of Landscape Architecture

The premise of this studio was that the distinction between garden and landscape is that with a garden the ideological foundations of the garden and the physical manifestation of these ideas in the form of the garden itself—whatever they might be—provide its defining experiential qualities. The distinction then, between landscape and garden, is the legibility of the intentions in the creation of the garden as an artifact. Critical to the understanding of this point of view is that all landscapes—whether gardens or natural—are living and dynamic natural systems. To reset in motion the processes of nature, without being accountable for making legible the intentions of the design of the landscape, is equal to deciding to not design at all. And although the idea of restarting or renewing natural processes without any legible marks of the designer's hand is certainly interesting and maybe even important, it was not the subject of this studio.

The core of our work was to transform the Service Parking Lot at Wellesley into a garden and a landscape for the sculpture collection of Ray and Patsy Nasher. Although the project itself is hypothetical, the collection is very real—destined for a new urban sculpture garden in Dallas. The site, of course, is also real, though it is not at all likely that the land as designated will be developed as a sculpture garden.

If it weren't for the fact that Ray Nasher has already decided to locate his collection next to the Dallas Museum of Art in Dallas, where he has lived most of his adult life, it is not absurd to think that Wellesley might develop this land as a sculpture garden. The site is located in close proximity to the Jewett Art Center and the Davis Museum and Cultural Center. The former design by Paul Rudolph and the latter by Rafael Moneo, are a connected pair of buildings yet they are remarkable examples of modern and contemporary architecture. Mr. Nasher was born and raised in Boston before moving to Dallas.

Although the Wellesley College landscape is generally an exceptionally beautiful place, the Service Lot is definitely the most degraded moment on the main campus. According to earlier master plans from the 1920s, the Service Lot was intended to be a vital and connected element of the campus's connected valley system. The site once had a small stream landscape that was obliterated at some point in this century when the current and massive parking lot was constructed on the site.

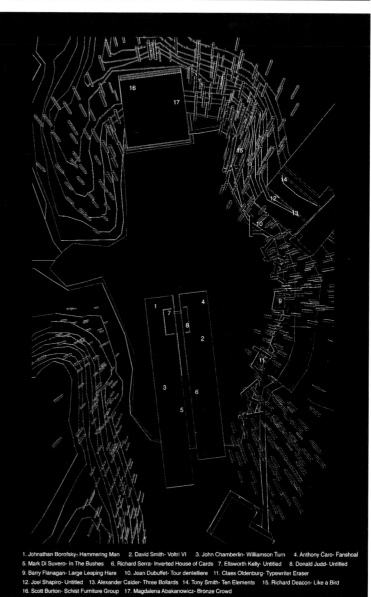

1. Johnathan Borofsky- Hammering Man   2. David Smith- Voltri VI   3. John Chamberlin- Williamson Turn   4. Anthony Caro- Fanshoal
5. Mark Di Suvero- In The Bushes   6. Richard Serra- Inverted House of Cards   7. Ellsworth Kelly- Untitled   8. Donald Judd- Untitled
9. Barry Flanagan- Large Leaping Hare   10. Jean Dubuffet- Tour dentelliere   11. Claes Oldenburg- Typewriter Eraser
12. Joel Shapiro- Untitled   13. Alexander Calder- Three Bollards   14. Tony Smith- Ten Elements   15. Richard Deacon- Like a Bird
16. Scott Burton- Schist Furniture Group   17. Magdalena Abakanowicz- Bronze Crowd

Roderick Wyllie MLA '98, Perspective View of
Sculpture Garden and Plan of Sculpture Placement

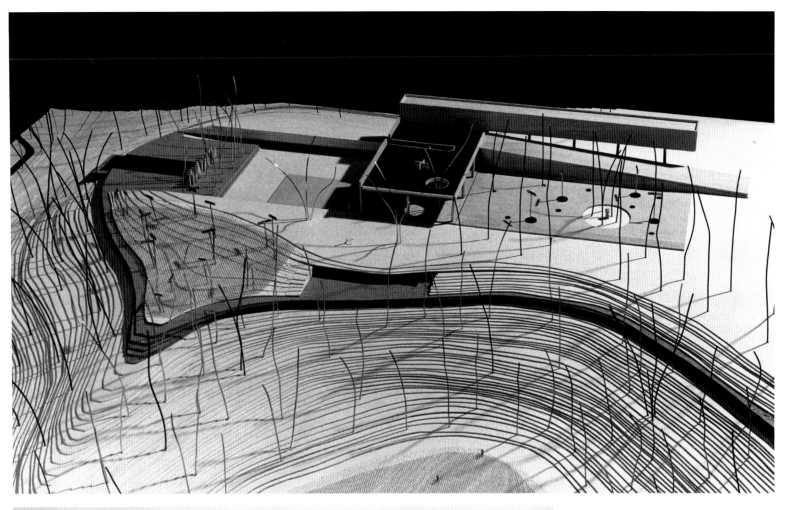

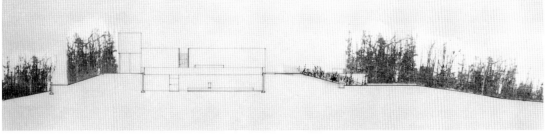

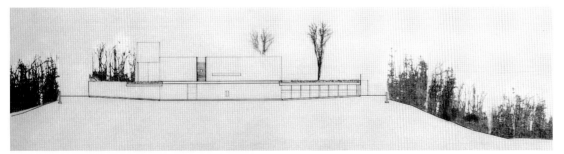

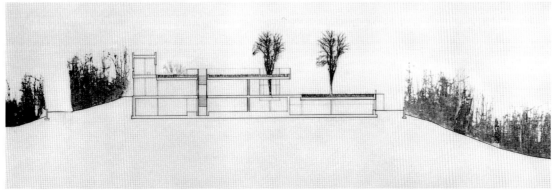

Emily Mueller MLA '98, Model View and Sections

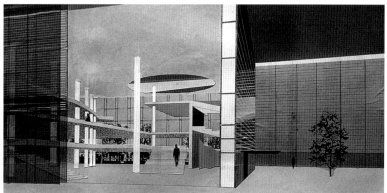

From Master Plan to Detail: The Development of Frankfurt University

Wilfried Wang
Adjunct Professor of Architecture

With the extensive changes in the wake of the reunification of Germany, the historically laden site of the former IG-Farben headquarters used prior to the Second World War by the once mighty chemical corporation and subsequently by the U.S. military—is to be developed on a long-term basis as a university facility inspired by North American university traditions (yard/campus).

The studio investigated the possibilities of merging the university's faculties along a long-term master plan and to provide a sample indication of one of its components. This included a section of landscape or a part of a building. Particular attention was paid to the current discourse on the spatial implications of pedagogy, resource management, and flexibility of facilities.

Extensive research was and will continue to be carried out along these lines both at the GSD as well as in Frankfurt. The projects are to be exhibited at the German Architecture Museum in December 1998.

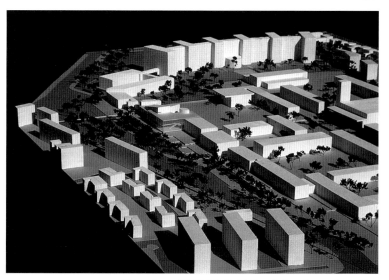

Osamu Sassa MAUD '99, Model View, Collage Perspective looking through the Auditorium Atrium, Model View showing Curtain Wall Detail from Entrance Plaza, and Model View of Master Plan

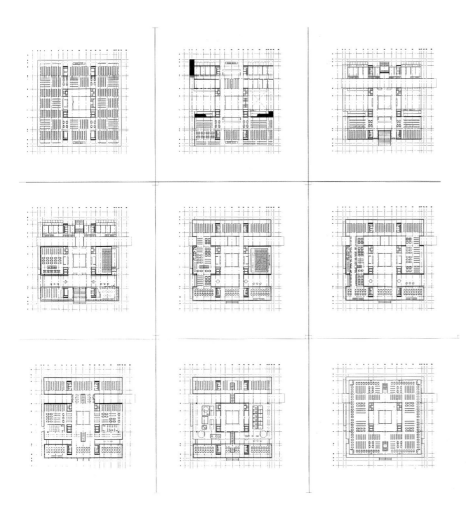

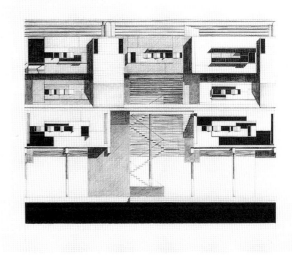

Andrew Junhoe Ku MArch '99, Plans, Model View, and Elevation

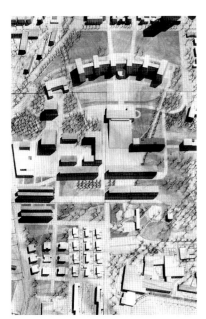

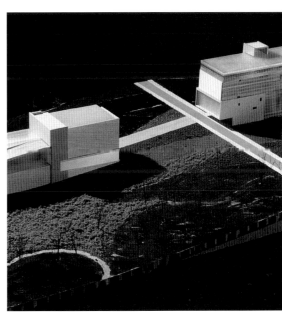

Jeeun Song MLA '98, Model of Master Plan, View from Roof Terrace, and Model View

A VAVDEVILLE THEATE

AND DANCE HALL

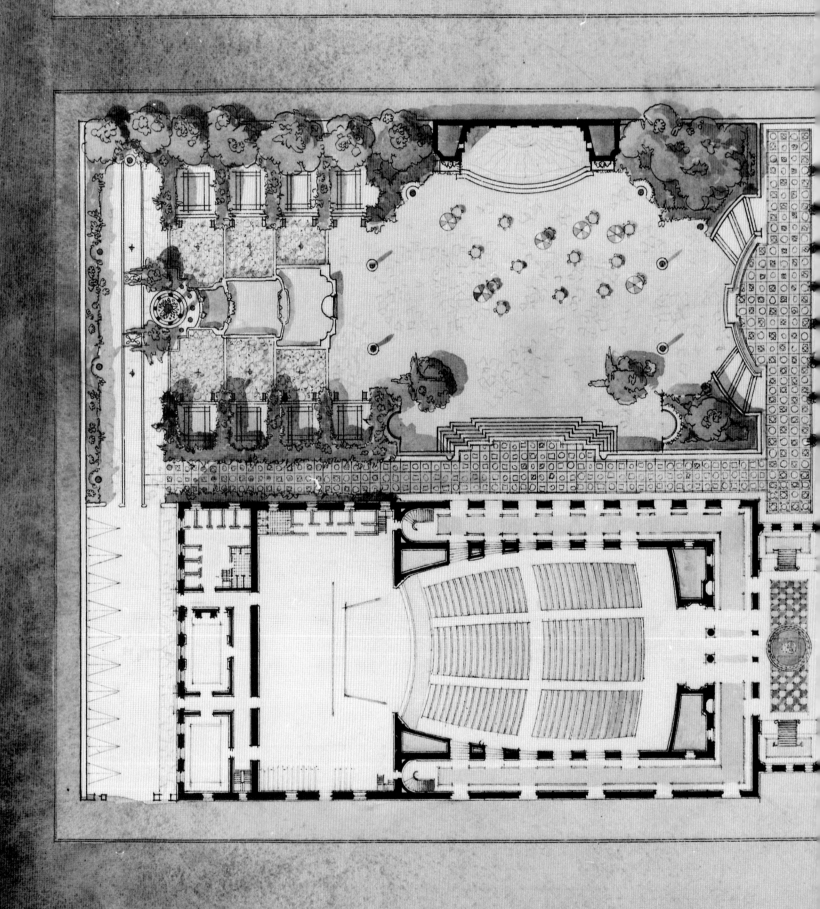

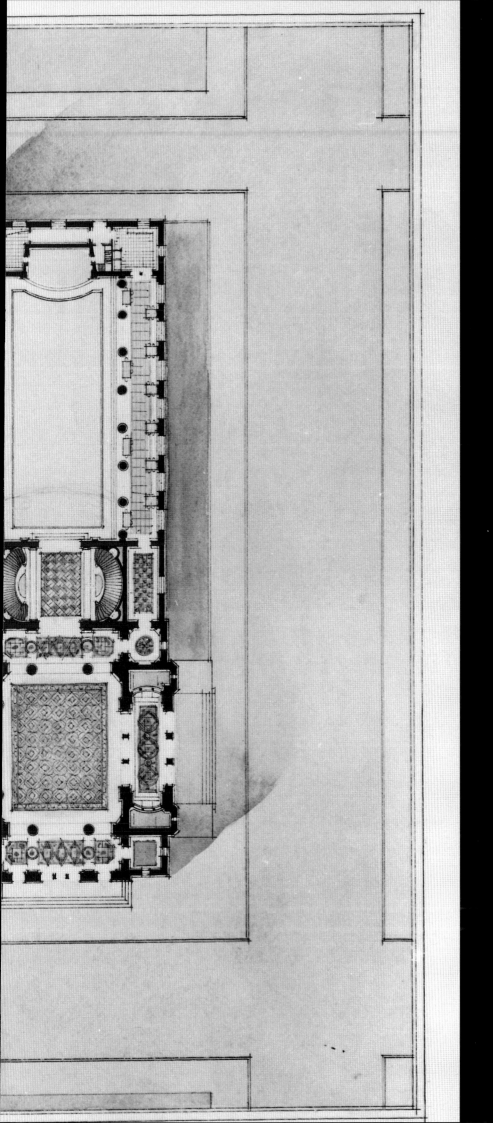

Aisner, Edward, "A
Vaudeville Theater and
Dance Hall," 1926. [Plan]
(Competition drawing; water
color on paper, 44x67 cm)

Outleaf: Morrison, Benjamin Y.,
A STUDY OF THE MINOR
ARCHITECTURAL FEATURES
OF CIVIC DECORATION . . .
1915. (Thesis NAC 3820 M83

A STUDY OF THE MINOR ARCHITECTURAL FEATURES OF CIVIC DECORATION: ESPECIALLY FOUNTAINS AND MONUMENTS . . . . . .

. . . A THESIS SUBMITTED IN LANDSCAPE ARCHITECTURE TEN · H · S · L · A · · JUNE NINETEEN HUNDRED FIFTEEN · BY · MORRISON

■ Fig. One.

Perspective from "A".

Perspective on either hand at "B"

Plan, perspective + cross perspective of an idealized straight street on level ground.

CONTEMPOVILLE

LOS ANGELES WORLD FAIR 1945.

SUBMITTED AS PART
OF A THESIS FOR THE
DEGREE MASTER OF
LANDSCAPE ARCHITEC
TURE AT THE GRAD
UATE SCHOOL OF DE
SIGN OF HARVARD
UNIVERSITY JUNE
17 1938 BY GARRETT
ECKBO

E

F

G

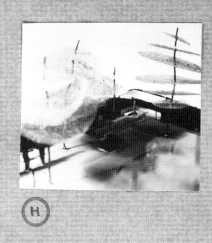

H

1   **2**   **3**

4   **5**   **6**

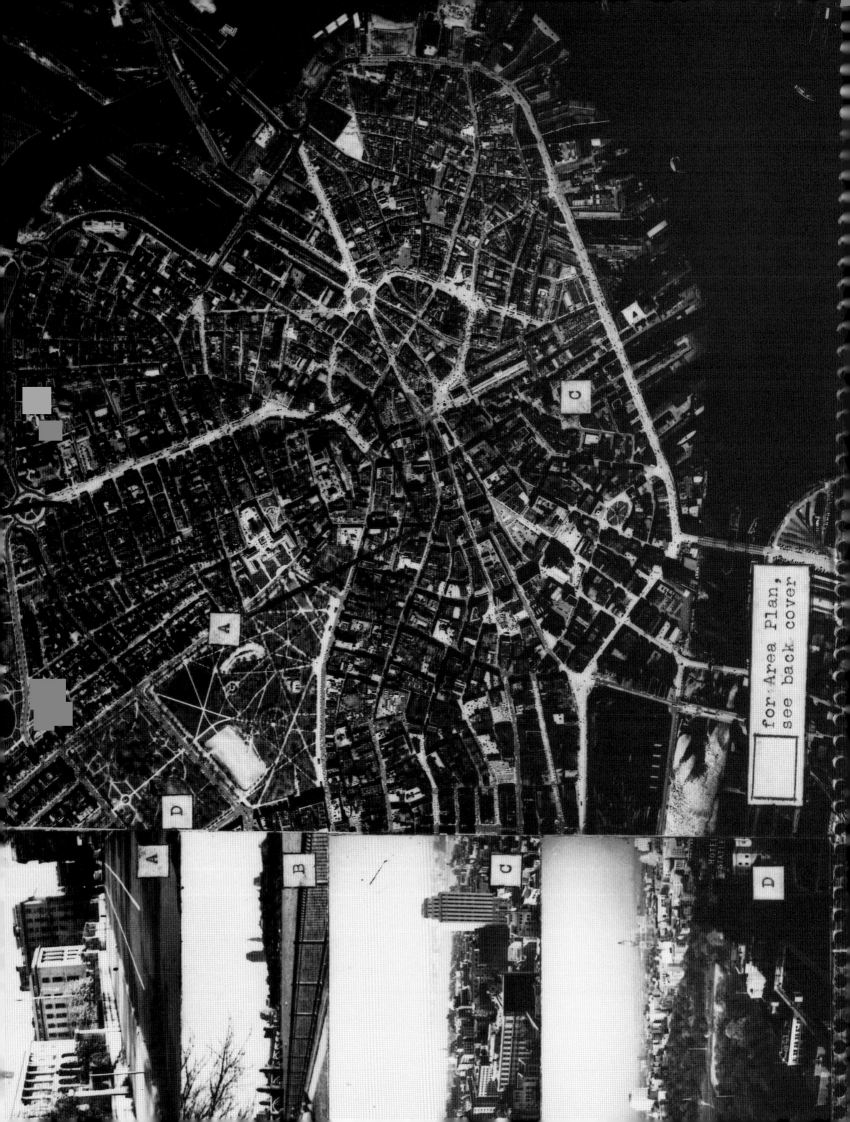

for Area Plan, see back cover

People demand freedom.

The state exists for the individual,
not the individual for the state.

If the state stands for conformity
and the individual for anarchy,
we must lean toward anarchy.

Boston needs a new City Hall.

Newspaper clippings dated 1901 show that the present structure
(finished in 1865) was even then considered obsolete.

Lack of action despite much talk has been due --

-- to the unsettled state of the City's political and
economic, and therefore financial, position; and --

-- to the lack of co-ordination among groups interested
in the City's overall plan, the lack of a master plan,
and therefore the lack of an agreed-upon site.

The conditions making for this inaction, while by no means near
an early solution, cannot be presumed to last indefinitely.

1. A comprehensive, feasible proposal for a new Boston
has been assumed as the first premise for this thesis
program. It is the first prize program in the Boston
Contest of 1944. The chief recommendations which bear
on the City Hall project are:

.   "The relative economic decline of New England
suggests a plan which lays stress on stability
rather than expansion."

.   A Metropolitan Authority, including the area within
a 20-mile radius of the State House, "to exercise
those joint functions which are clearly metropolitan
in nature." It would be of the city manager type.

.   A property tax based on the fair value of the land,
not including buildings, in order not to penalize
improvements through new building.

.   A transportation system based on the "private motor

Sturgis, R. S. BOSTON CITY
HALL, 1950–1951. (Student

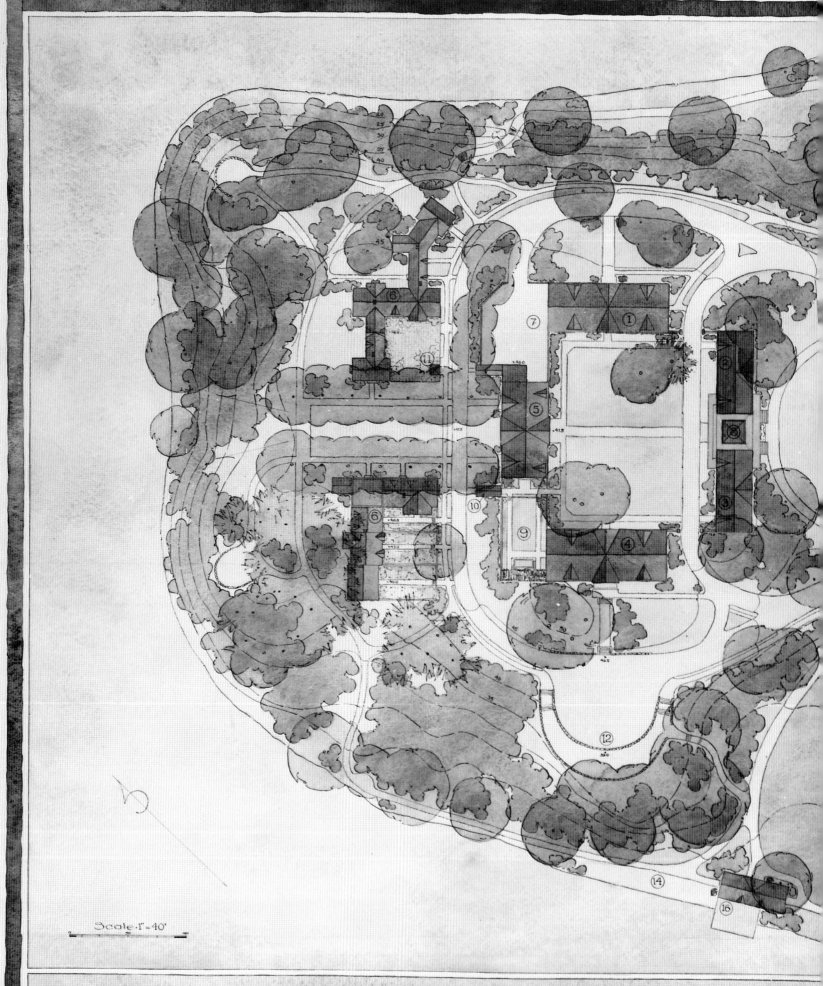

Scale·1"=40'

AN ARTS AND CRAFTS

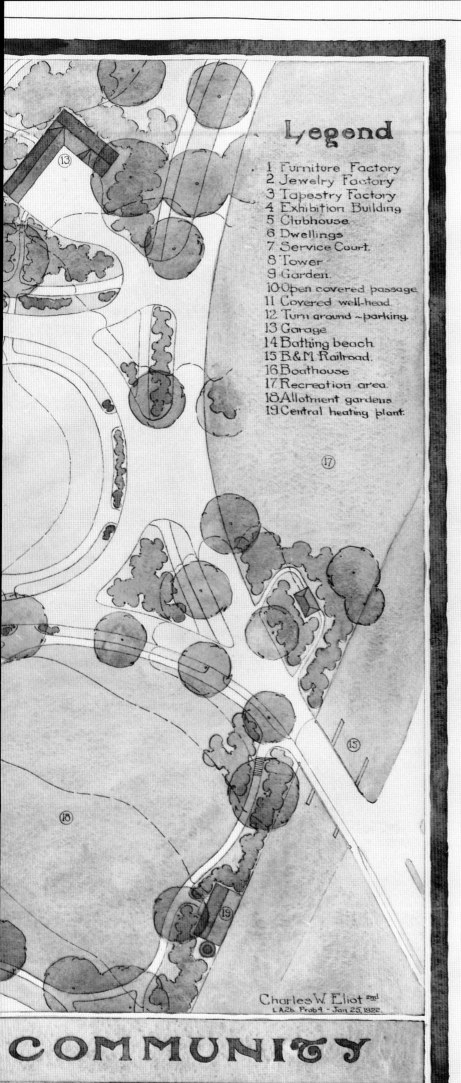

Legend

1 Furniture Factory
2 Jewelry Factory
3 Tapestry Factory
4 Exhibition Building
5 Clubhouse
6 Dwellings
7 Service Court
8 Tower
9 Garden
10 Open covered passage
11 Covered well-head
12 Turn around ~ parking
13 Garage
14 Bathing beach
15 B.&M. Railroad
16 Boathouse
17 Recreation area
18 Allotment gardens
19 Central heating plant

Charles W. Eliot 2nd
L.A.2b. Prob 4 - Jan 25, 1922.

COMMUNITY

THESIS

RESOLUTION PASSED BY THE STUDENTS OF THE GRADUATE SCHOOL OF DESIGN, APRIL 10, 1969

RESOLVED:

GSD students will abstain from any official school activity until Monday night April 14.

This strike is in outrage against the use of police power at University Hall and in protest against the arbitrary concentration of power in the hands of the President and Fellows of Harvard College.

The time will be used for study and discussion of proposals, demands and actions for the coming months.

We are in sympathy and in support of the "Resolution Passed by the Memorial Church Meeting, April 10, 1969."

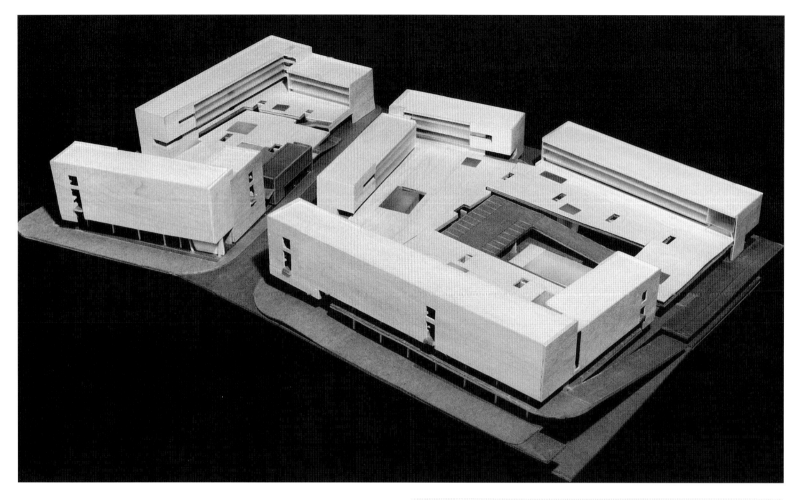

Alexandra Barker

MArch I

Supra-Market Living

This thesis project combines housing with a supermarket in a city block located at the boundary between two Boston neighborhoods, Roxbury and the South End. The block occupies the northwest corner of the intersection of Melnea Cass Boulevard, a future link in Boston's proposed Urban Ring project, with Washington Street, a historic transportation artery in an area currently undergoing rehabilitation with ample opportunities for development.

Through the integration of housing with an expanded supermarket and retail program within a single volume, the thesis proposes an architecture that addresses theoretical and philosophical issues raised in research about contemporary urban social conditions. These conditions are described as complex social interactions of people who 'map' their place in the world through their everyday movements and encounters. The resulting contrasting understandings of the space of the building as one moved through it, either as a shopper or as a resident, provided a means of investigating the primary focus of my thesis—the presence of the subject in architecture, where I addressed both the presence of the human subject in a space for inhabitation as well as subjectivity—situational and material particularity and its relationship to rationalizing, abstracting tendencies of theoretical and scientific systems of knowledge.

Advisor
George Baird

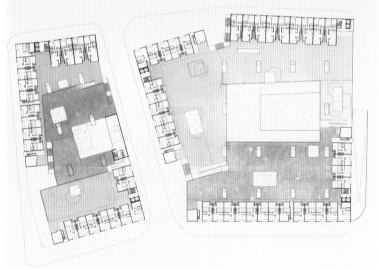

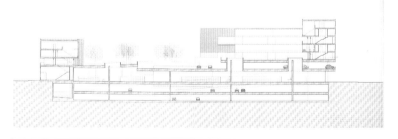

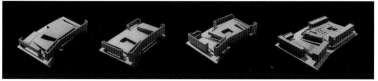

Model View, Second Floor Plan, Longitudinal Section, and Model Views

Sketch of Stuttgart Station by R. Nagle, Stuttgart, 1914-24; Autobahn Bridge designed by Paul Bonatz, Limburg, 1938-40; Sketch of Single Arch by Paul Bonatz, Pergamon, 1952; and Transformation of the Single Arch of the Stuttgart Train Station

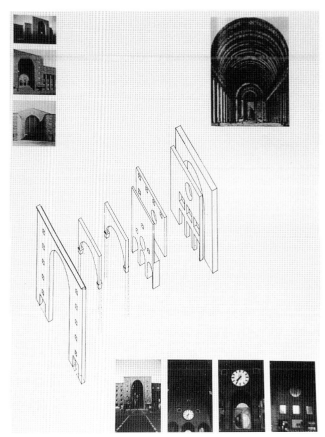

Zeynep Celik
MArch I

Paul Bonatz (1877–1956): Rethinking the Pre-Fascist Topography of German Architecture

The persistence of the arch in the work of Paul Bonatz is unmistakable. The isolated single arch appears recurrently in Bonatz's travel sketches as the last traces of a lost prehistoric harmony. His schemes for the Autobahn bridges of the Third Reich, on the other hand, are constituted by the obsessive iteration of the exact same arch. Why then do the arches of the Stuttgart Train Station refuse to connect and to become a bridge? The single arches along the facade of the colossal building persevere in the imagistic power of their simplicity as distinct arches.

Here the specific strategy of ordering employed by Bonatz is not that of simple iteration; rather, he uses a subtle architectural device, which I have called seriality, to mediate between the Gestalt of the exterior arch and its particularized interior versions. The single arch undergoes a transformation whereby its scale, texture, and materials become gradually more differentiated.

This not only corresponds to Bonatz's strategy of wrapping a mute shell around the highly particularized bourgeois residential interior of the nineteenth century, but to the reconciliatory role that Bonatz assumes in the face of antagonistic forces in general. Bonatz registers "the sickness of modern times," like so many of his contemporaries, but chooses to disguise the sickness under a spider's web. While inventing highly creative architectural strategies of preserving accepted cultural forms, Bonatz complies with a fascism that seeks to disrupt the bourgeois culture in which those forms are structurally embedded.

Advisor
K. Michael Hays

Choon Choi

MArch I

Plasticitis: Monsanto House of the Future

Plastic in architecture, perceived as a cultural phenomenon as well as a material intervention, resists any coherent conceptualization of its historical significance. It escapes our attempts to place it in a specific and intelligible context, and affirms its ambiguous identity as material and metaphor. The aim of this thesis was to illuminate plastic's shifting relation to the given historical moment, its contributions to contemporary culture, and the changing debates within modernism, of which plastic was an involuntary agent. The thesis examined the question of whether plastic's influence on architecture ever transcended its commercial value, or whether the public was simply the unsuspecting victim of subversive corporate hype, which architects wisely ignored. This study, however, was not an attempt to defend the usefulness of plastic against the reluctance of the building industry to adopt it, or to provide a conclusive explanation for the failure of the visionary ventures in the past to plasticize our environment. Rather, the study was a form of diagnosis of the post-war American culture to which plastic projects in architecture emerged as a response. Ultimately, it is hoped that such a diagnosis will establish a critical frame through which we can relate the many cultural ramifications of plastic to the changing perception of modernism.

Advisor

Sarah Ksaizek

Photomontage, Construction View of Monsanto House of the Future, and Completed House at Disneyland

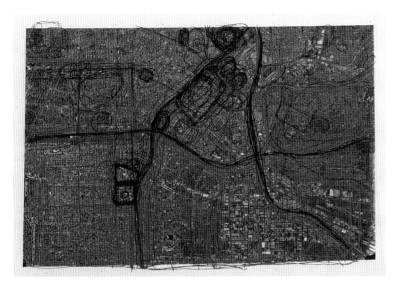

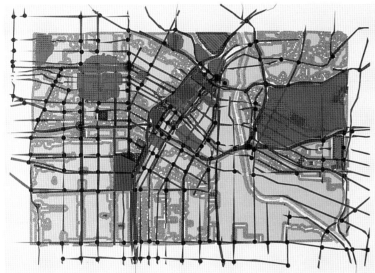

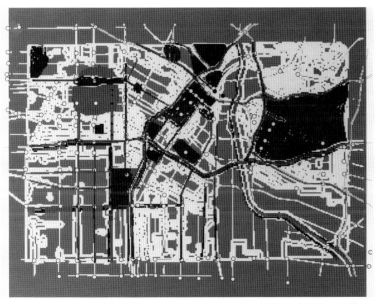

Layered Map made from a compilation of thiry-five Data Survey Maps,
Comparison Map: City/Mosaic Composite, Diagnostic Map: Intervention Areas

Thomas Cody
MUP

The Urban Mosaic

The thesis proposes that the investigation of two theories and methods—one urban and one ecological—and their application to a common site can collapse the conventional filters and boundaries between the natural and built disciplines. By doing so, the complementary nature of two normally opposed arenas can then be illustrated.

The planning and design of built systems are improved and efficiently advanced with the application of established facts and theories pertaining to natural systems. Specifically, employing ecological, evolutionary, and biological sciences reveals insights regarding the interaction, relationships, and spatial organization of fragmented communities in a modern urban context. Kevin Lynch, in the realm of urban planning, and Richard Forman, in that of landscape ecology, have been pivotal in the advancement of their respective fields. They have independently produced theories and models for analyzing, describing, and ordering built and natural systems. Although they have produced their models and theories to address diametrically opposed systems, both Lynch's and Forman's models are markedly similar.

Both the urban and ecological models consist of five elements situated within a bigger medium. Lynch's urban model incorporates districts, landmarks, paths, nodes, and edges in the larger city. The ecological model generated by Forman brings patches, outliners, corridors, intersections, and edges together within a matrix. I have adapted the models and theories from Lynch's *The Image of the City* and Forman's *Land Mosaics* and applied them to a common site: an area roughly five by seven miles in central Los Angeles.

The result is one description of the site according to my interpretation of Lynch's method and one description based on my adaptation of the landscape ecology method. The models can be compared and analyzed according to these descriptions. The evaluated conclusions from such a site reveal that the functions of a city can be inferred from methods based on visual form which, in turn, are based on the functioning of ecosystems. Most importantly, the ecological model presents interesting and highly relevant theoretical and factual results for city planning and design. The application of established theories of natural systems may improve and efficiently advance the planning and design of built systems.

Advisor
Carl Steinitz

Adib Curé and Carie Penabad
MAUD

Miami: A Case Study in Visual Planning

While the forces that shape the modern city are both varied and complex, it is certain that in recent history economical/functional concerns have become the overriding generating forces of design. This reality has provided an impoverished view of the city, which has far too often produced redundant, homogenized urban landscapes. In response to this seemingly bleak urban condition, the thesis set out to question a mode of investigation centered on a scenographic or visual understanding of the city. Consequently, the thesis proposed to analyze a visual planning strategy that does not rely on the plan as point of departure, but rather begins with an understanding of the city in elevation and perspective. Therefore, the investigation is not concerned with an abstract two-dimensional understanding of the plan, but rather proceeds to elaborate and structure the plan based on visual and formal characteristics of existing conditions.

In order to arrive at a scenographic understanding of the city based on the vertical plane, a precise methodology needs to be employed that relies on the determination of a series of public viewing points from which visual sight lines of actual significance can be determined. It is from these predetermined vantage points that a series of highly scenographic views can be composed through the careful manipulation of foreground, middleground, and background elements. Moreover, it should be stated that the thesis sought to explore two modes of visual perception, the scenographic and the picturesque, in order to facilitate a visual framework for interventions within the city. Scenography is intrinsically linked to the fixed and a priori position of the spectator in space while the picturesque relies on a more dynamic conception of space based on the notion of infinite transformation that presupposes the variable points of view of a moving spectator. This conception of space is above all a struggle against the reduction of "all terrains" to the flatness of a piece of paper, and ultimately suggests a liberation between the elevation and the plan.

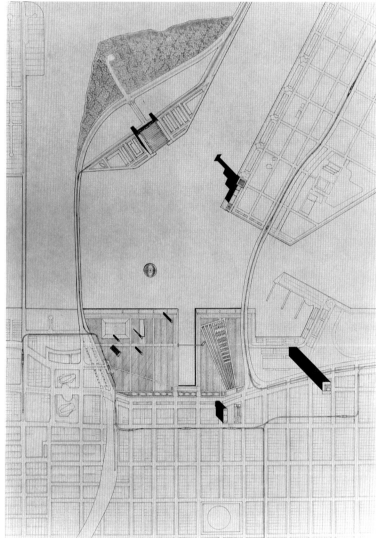

Perspective View from Watson Island toward Downtown Miami, Biscayne Bay Site Plan

Advisors
Rodolphe el-Khoury
Rodolfo Machado

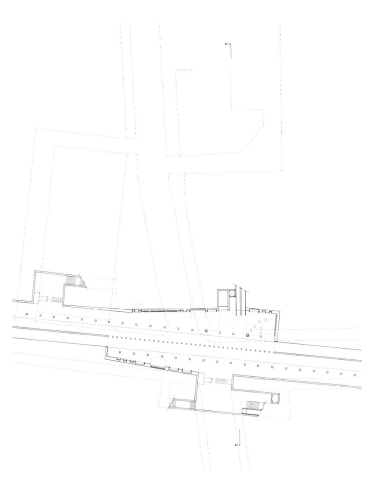

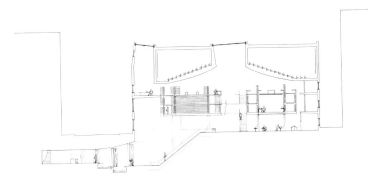

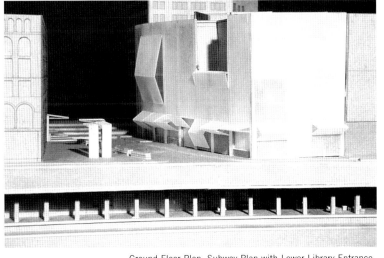

Ground Floor Plan, Subway Plan with Lower Library Entrance,
Section through Chinatown Subway Stop, and Model View

Kim K. Elliott
MArch I

Paradox: a library

> Paradox: The integration of things with seemingly
> contradictory qualities or phases.

By combining contradictory qualities, new spaces are invented through moments of overlap, shared programmatic areas, and juxtaposition with existing elements. The library program becomes the vehicle to investigate how paradoxes such as the book and the computer, light and dark spaces, civic and mundane, and commercial versus intellectual browsing can co-exist.

The library carves out a corner of an existing retail building and movie theater directly above a subway stop situated at the edge of Chinatown and at the end of the busy downtown shopping district in Boston. The three architectural strategies that integrated several paradoxical conditions in order to reinvent the "expected" library are: the electrification of the library (an electrical wall that unfolds through the building—a combination of the book and the computer), the need for extremely different light conditions, and the extension of the library to allow for kiosks, newsstands, the subway platform, and a cinema.

Advisor
Sheila Kennedy

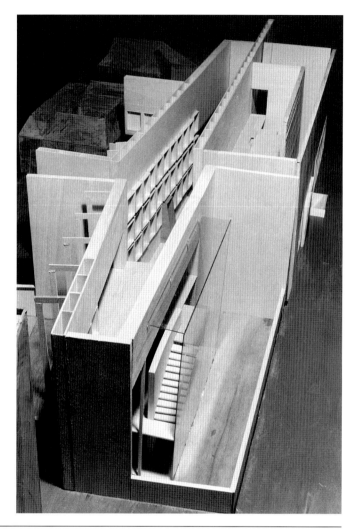

Leekyung Han
MArch I

The Alley

Printed words hold memories, ideas and plans.
Books are the containers of this historical corpus.
And libraries and bookstores make accessible to
the reader, the books, words, memories and concepts....

Michael Spens

Insadong, in Seoul, South Korea, is a repository of historical and cultural layers. The accumulated layers, not easily noticeable from the main road, begin to reveal themselves in the labyrinth-like alley structures and let one unlock the memories associated with them—for example, finding a traditional housing fabric and experiencing it recalls past memories. Constant phenomenal travel between past and present in Insadong makes the whole area a "memory museum." This experience is condensed and translated into a rare book library/bookstore. An alley housing chronologically exhibited books of unique quality in a pristine book stack becomes the bookstore, and the rare book library subdivided by subject into several volumes is created in the same way that houses and an alley are formed.

Advisor
Darell Fields

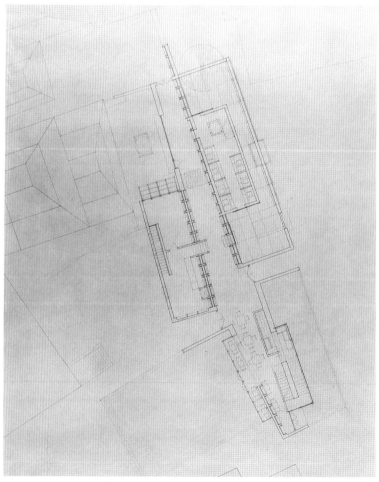

Model View, Perspective View of the Bookstore: The Alley, and Plan

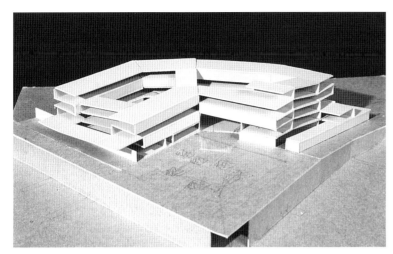

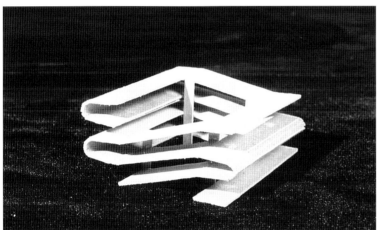

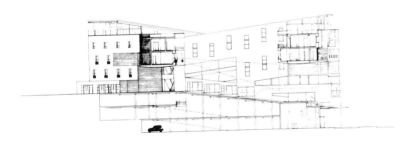

Schematic Model View, Study Model View, Section, and Facade Detail

Zachary Hinchliffe
MArch I

Hotel/Housing Complex: Rabat, Morocco

> Strangely the foreigner lives within us: he is the
> hidden face of our identity, the space that wrecks
> our abode, the time in which understanding and
> affinity founder.
>
> Julia Kristeva, *Strangers to Ourselves*

The thesis attempted to address issues of post-colonial identity in an architectural manner. The characteristic hybridity of post-colonial cities is a condition that precludes synthesis; what is apparent is the coexistence of difference rather than the assimilation or reconciliation of foreignness. The project aimed to mirror this condition, not the popular image of Moroccan identity fueled by fantasy and nostalgia. "Authenticity" is revealed to be inevitably false as it seeks to make seamless that which has been torn apart.

The city of Rabat is split between the pre-colonial city, the medina, and the Ville Nouvelle built by the French. Contemporary urban development is characterized by a radical peripheralization. The history of housing projects in Morocco is interesting within this framework because it demonstrates the tensions and ambiguities of both the colonial and post-colonial period. The desire to create synthetic medinas apparent in the "new medinas" of the early Protectorate period (1912–1925) gave way to the modernist aspirations of the period just prior to Moroccan independence (1948–1956). Most visibly in the projects from the 1950s, modernity was mutated by the desire to integrate the most emblematic feature of Islamic architecture, the courtyard, and thereby respond to the paramount feature of sociological difference, the need for absolute privacy.

The project's site was an area of Rabat's medina that currently houses a marginalized population living in a shantytown. It is adjacent to an active shopping street with heavy tourist traffic. The municipality of Rabat has long been interested in developing additional tourism in the area. Given this condition, the project aimed to satisfy the prerogative of development without displacing the existing residents.

One can imagine the project as a parking garage that keeps the cars entering from different sides. The two programs occupy the same building, yet are segregated in their circulation. In plan, section, and elevation one program figures the other in an endless Gestalt operation. The awareness of otherness (the other desired and feared by the tourist, the other envied and scorned by the native) is always present. It is not a mixed-use development, but rather the entire building is simultaneously a hotel and a housing project.

Advisor
Rodolphe el-Khoury

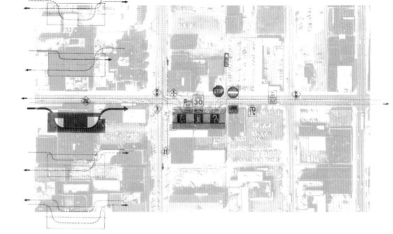

Tien-Lun Ho
MArch I

Condition: Terminal

Perhaps one of the most inevitable by-products of the post-industrial age is the desuetude and abandonment of industrial sites. This thesis investigates the potential reinterpretation of such abandoned sites in a deteriorating city. Through the process of analysis, my research documented the urban condition at Lima, Ohio, then examined the inextricably intertwining relationship between technology and landscape, and finally offered a solution of urban re-occupation. The goal was to propose a site and a program that would reinvest Lima with an alternative sense of meaning and viability as a post-industrial city.

Present-day Lima is in a critical state of decline. The city, once a central hub of industrial manufacturing and energy production, now solely receives and then transforms raw materials from outside sources. Lima's infrastructural systems that have either been decommissioned or scheduled for shutdown offered a framework for analysis.

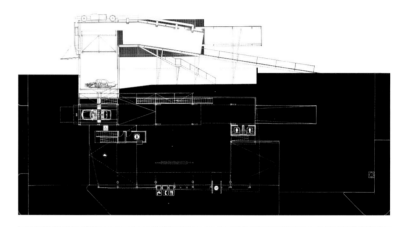

A gas station prototype was proposed as a programmatic intervention to reflect the city's ruptures and to acknowledge the unrealized potential of industrial infrastructure as a plausible instrument of salvation. A vacant parking lot on the intersection of North and Main Street, which interfaces between the central business district and the highway, was chosen as a typical corner condition.

The design of the gas terminal espouses a functionalist, hard-edged, machine aesthetic that expresses an ambiguous vision of technology. The primary design strategy for the gas station provides both vertical and elevated infrastructure. The station, along with automated wash tunnel, gas pumps, and mechanical support spaces, is raised above ground and vehicles drive down below for other auto services. The resulting space between the roof and the underpass provides daylight and ventilation for heat and gas vapor.

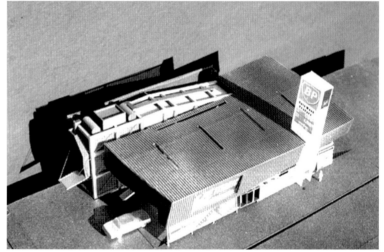

A 35-foot-tall translucent glass sign, also serving as a bus shelter would draw motorists from a far distance. However, it is the abstracted scale of the rustic metal deck roof that becomes the eye-catching icon for motorists—a recognizable logo for this particular chain of gas stations. At street level, an electronic transaction wall containing many transient programs allows the general public to "plug" themselves in for all types of transactions. At night, a reverse effect occurs, the digital wall along with the 35-foot- tower is lit up to serve as a luminous "sign" while the roof becomes a darkened backdrop. The entire station becomes its own billboard or "sign." Or rather, the image of the gas station is treated almost as a historical ruin, its construction reassembled out of the detritus of Lima's industrialization.

Advisor

Toshiko Mori

Site Plan: Circulation Diagrams, Plan and Longitudinal Section,
Model View, and Interior Model View

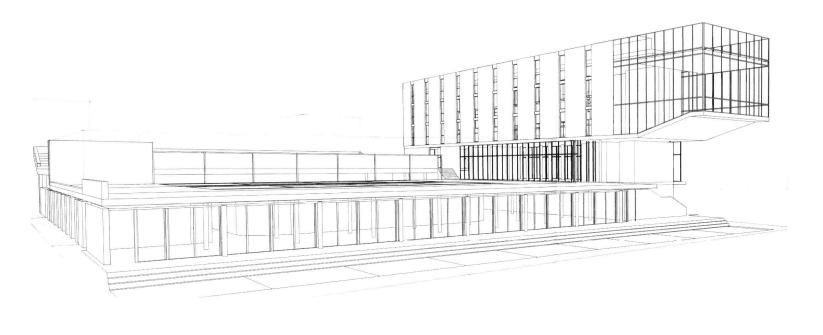

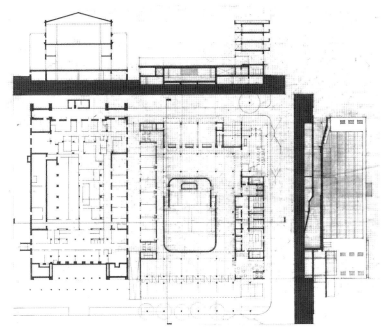

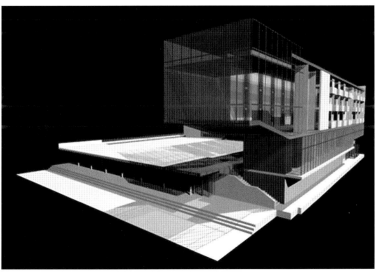

Karen Lu
MARCH I

Campus Infill

Campus infill is a contemporary response toward campus architecture and planning. Such buildings occupy sites that are located within existing campus boundaries. In order to address qualitative concerns of campus life, campus infill buildings often maintain strong relationships to existing circulation patterns, landscaped courts, and adjacent functions and structures. This thesis project, a faculty center, establishes a foundation of social activity and interaction at the Massachusetts Institute of Technology through the overlapping of spatial and programmatic concerns.

Currently, the site is occupied by MIT's East Campus Tennis Courts, located on the Charles River. The project's massing and resulting distribution of program respond to a unique site condition of student dormitories and the President's House, surrounded by numerous academic buildings. Decisions concerning site and program have also evolved in reaction to current and historical trends in MIT's educational and institutional policy, and in consideration of future campus planning and development to the east.

The faculty center's ground floor contains classrooms, lounges, and a large lecture hall. As a result, the existing tennis courts have been relocated onto the roof of this "plinth." A public dining facility, at the level of the tennis courts, serves to connect the plinth with the faculty center's residences, a long rectilinear mass on Ames Street. The resulting form, together with adjacent buildings, allows for a multiple reading of exterior spaces and programmatic associations. The faculty center will establish a forum for visiting faculty to interact with the MIT community by allowing them not only to contribute, but also to disseminate knowledge.

Advisor
Carol Burns

Perspective View from Memorial Drive, Study Sketch with Plan and Sections, and Perspective View from Ames Street and Memorial Drive

City of Shopping.

The city proper has twice suffered ignobilities at the hand of the suburbs; once upon the loss of its constituency to the suburbs, and again upon that constituency's return. These prodigal citizens brought back with them their new desires for control and predictability.

Post-Mall Urbanism

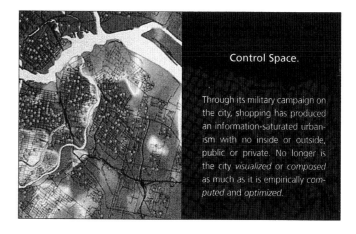

Control Space.

Through its military campaign on the city, shopping has produced an information-saturated urbanism with no inside or outside, public or private. No longer is the city *visualized* or *composed* as much as it is empirically *computed* and *optimized.*

Tae-Wook Cha MLA II

Jutiki Gunter MArch II

Daniel Herman MArch I

Hiromi Hosoya MArch I

Juan Palop-Casado MDesS

Sze Tsung Leong MArch I

Kiwa Matsushita MArch I

John McMorrough MArch II

Markus Schaefer MArch I

Tran Vinh MArch I

Srdjan Jovanovich Weiss MArch II

Louise Wyman MLA I

with:

Nicole Gaenzler MLA '97

Teng-Wui Leong MAUD '97

Jeffrey Inaba, Teaching Fellow

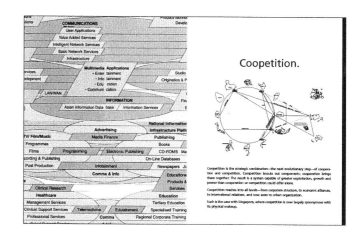

Coopetition.

Coopetition is the strategic combination—the next evolutionary step—of cooperation and competition. Competition knocks out components; coopetition brings them together. The result is a system capable of greater exploitation, growth and power than cooperation or competition could offer alone.

Coopetition reaches into all levels—from corporate structure, to economic alliances, to international relations, and now even to urban organization.

Such is the case with Singapore, where coopetition is now largely synonymous with its physical makeup.

Project on the City: Shopping

The Project on the City is a multi-year research undertaking that studies the effects of modernization on the contemporary city. The focus of the second year of this project is shopping—a field that not only operates according to its own internal paradigms, logic, and language, but remains mostly invisible to academic inquiry. In researching shopping, what is revealed is an urbanism that is more prolific, more powerful, more efficient, and responsible for an exponentially greater percentage of urban fabric than any of the "official" realms of architecture and urbanism. With increasing sophistication, mutability, parasitism, and desperation, shopping is proliferating to the point that it is becoming analogous to the development of the city—to the point that modernization must now be understood in terms of shopping.

Advisor
Rem Koolhaas

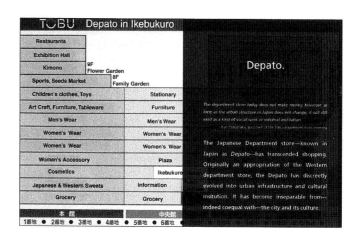

Depato.

The department store today does not make money. However, as long as the urban structure in Japan does not change, it will still exist as a kind of social asset or cultural institution.
— Ei Tamechika, president of the Tobu department store company

The Japanese Department store—known in Japan as *Depato*—has transcended shopping. Originally an appropriation of the Western department store, the Depato has discreetly evolved into urban infrastructure and cultural institution. It has become inseparable from—indeed coequal with—the city and its culture.

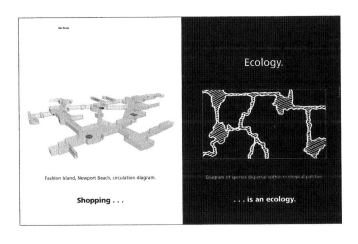

Ecology.

Fashion Island, Newport Beach, circulation diagram.

Diagram of species dispersal within ecological patches

Shopping . . .

. . . is an ecology.

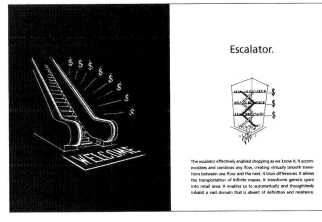

Escalator.

The escalator effectively enabled shopping as we know it. It accommodates and combines any flow, creating virtually smooth transitions between one floor and the next. It blurs differences. It allows the transportation of infinite masses. It transforms generic space into retail area. It enables us to automatically and thoughtlessly inhabit a vast domain that is absent of definition and resistance.

The Next Big Thing.

The Next Big Thing is always on the way. If you don't like this one, just wait until the next one. Though, of course, satisfaction is not guaranteed.

Architecture was never so lively, and never so crude. This is the architecture of shopping. It is unstable, always in transition. It is obvious in its tactics, but confident in its ability to seduce, for however brief an interlude.

Shopping architecture is not meant to be seen. It is gauged not by the eye, but by the *statistic*. The numerical demands of the market—volume, turnover, expansion, gain—give architectural form to shopping. This now inviolate market has long since overtaken America.

The department store, the mall, even the big box--they're dead and buried. Wait'll you see The Next Big Thing.

NikeTowns.

Replascape.

Replascape: 1. Nature technologically improved to stimulate commerce. 2. Organic material mechanically restructured, technically optimized, hypernaturalized, unrestrained by climate, duplicated at will. 3. The exquisitely logical yet perverse endproduct of modernization.

Resistance.

In Europe, it's shopping vs. the city.

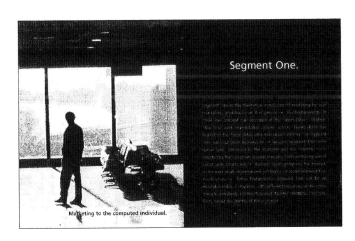

Segment One.

Marketing to the computed individual.

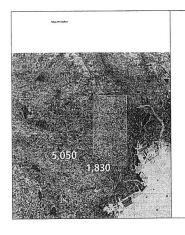

Tokyo Metabolism.

The Japanese convenience store

The Japanese Convenience Store is **the ultimate metabolist project**. Akin to systems engineering rather than architectural design, it combines the virtues of brand identity, just-in-time delivery and a highly computerized system for store inventory and consumer profiles into a **network of distributed architecture**, decentralized "point" stores in the city of which are fine-tuned to customer preferences in their specific neighborhoods. By affecting real estate and rents even as slightly, while being **highly mobile** due to comparatively low investment, the stores consume a **flexible field of urban magnets**. The store inventory is also well adjusted to the needs of the individual urbanite that it constitutes a **panopticon** of daily life, emanating reassurance and pleasure in its ordered deviate, as well as the most subtle seduction of convenience agent. The system represents **an urban organism** which is distributed, **networked**, highly **adaptive** and **intelligent**. Its urban presence is pure process - a metabolist's dream.

5,050

1,830

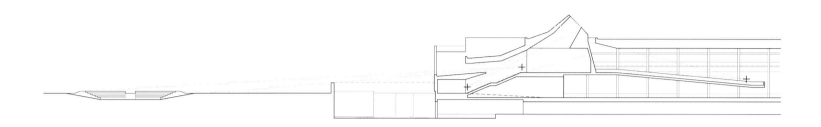

Michael Price
MArch I

Relative Viewpoints (On the Border)

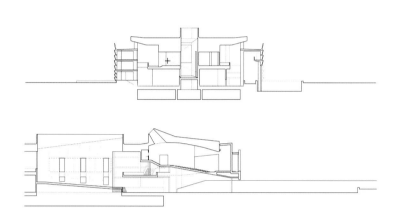

The powers of perception limit one's ability to fully comprehend the environment. The temporal and spatial continuity of the general experience disguises the fact that at any single moment one can only see a fragment of the surroundings. We acquire comprehensive understandings of the objects and spaces we encounter only through the summation of overlapping partial perceptions (or images). The knowledge of any "whole" results from a mental process of editing and integrating these visual fragments. Consequently, when multiple perceptions fail to neatly coalesce within one's mind, comprehension of the totalities becomes elusive, and what one beholds appears ambiguous.

This phenomenon has interesting implications for architecture. Because the visual experience of architecture is based on collections of blurred "snapshots," it is inherently immersed in this dialectic between fragments and understandings of totality. If different images of an architectural construct contain contradictory information, the fundamental identity of that architecture becomes ambiguous. Confusion arises as the viewer's expectations are undermined from one viewing position to the next.

This thesis attempted to explore and exploit architecture's potential to yield multiple readings, or "truths," to an observer. The project, a center for trade and cultural exchange, straddles the Mexican-American border in the desert west of El Paso, Texas. In this region several distinct, yet interdependent, cultural heritages converge with those of the United States and Mexico, as well as local Native American cultures. Within this context, the political border exists as an artificial, and paradoxical, intervention. The simple singularity of its monumental gesture disguises its sublime complexity. As a barrier, it exemplifies how a dominant ideology can profoundly impact the physical environment and consequently, society.

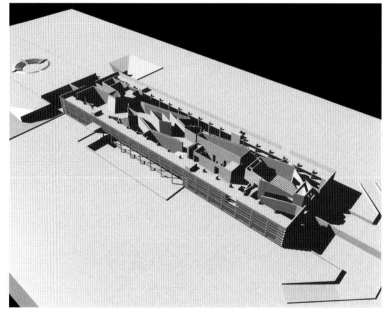

Sections and Computer Model View

To evoke multiple readings of the Mexican-American border, the project utilized phenomena of visual ambiguity. Predetermined sequences of visual effects were intertwined and fused together, generating the architectural morphology. The result is a connection between viewpoint and image that corresponds to anamorphism. One's movement through the building triggers seemingly irreconcilable moments of experience. The occupant arrives at different understandings from contrasting viewpoints, which frustrates any attempts to rationalize the scene. Many "partial-truths" subvert the notion of an absolute, dominant, or privileged point of view. A sense of the border as incomprehensible or irreducible is ultimately conveyed.

Advisor
Monica Ponce de Leon

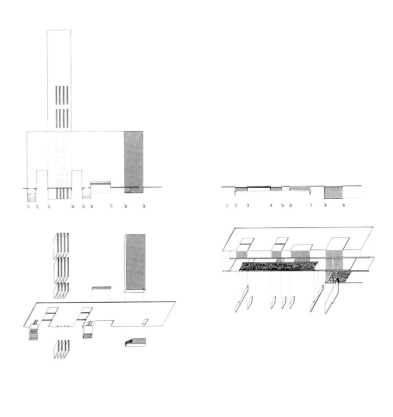

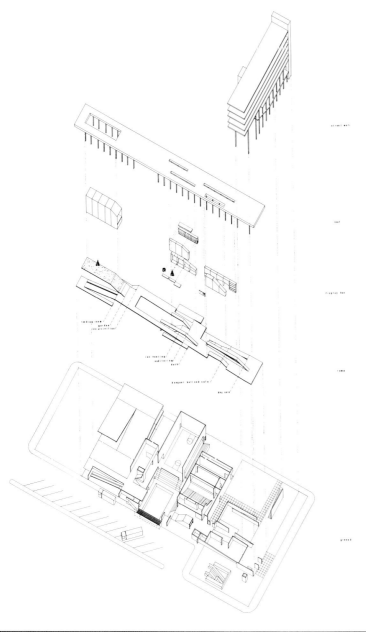

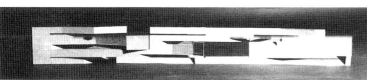

Accessibility and Visibility Diagram, Exploded Axonometric View,
Lobby Bar Model: Fluttering Strip, and Model Views

Patricia Rhee
MArch I

Establishing a Presence:
An Orientation Center in Koreatown, Los Angeles

The thesis examined and attempted to alleviate the physical, political, and cultural tensions brought about by the encroachment of Koreatown onto the older fabric of establishment Los Angeles. Characterized by cosmetic renovation and the haphazard signage of individual tenants, the growth of Koreatown along Western Avenue is at odds with the controlled civic image of Wilshire Boulevard. The site lies at the uneasy intersection of these two streets.

The thesis proposes an orientation center consisting of cultural and community components, along with a bus terminal and subway station—the pairings that reflect the dualistic nature of the site. The deliberate location and interweaving of these new programmatic elements tries to subvert their conventional placement on Wilshire Boulevard or Western Avenue. The Orientation Center thus expresses the collision of the two urban conditions and establishes the presence of Koreatown on Wilshire without privileging the character of one over the other. A linear lobby and gallery space, the "civic" bar, links community center programs and outdoor gardens through ramps, stairs, and walkways. An architecture of arrival, orientation, and access weaves two formerly distinct urban fabrics and provides a hybridized public space appropriate for the particular conditions of the site.

Advisor
Monica Ponce de Leon

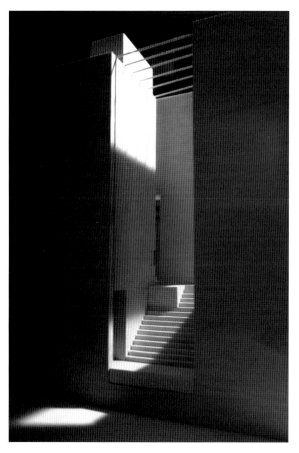

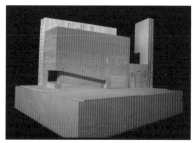

Eric Stark

MArch I

The Great Jones Shadow Puppet Theater

The concept for the puppet theater arose from contradictions inherent in the Javanese shadow puppet. A thin, finely crafted buffalo hide is brightly painted and gilded, yet this colorful object is used to cast a black shadow onto a white canvas screen. Contradictions between light and shadow, the physical and the ephemeral, scales, and cultures permeate the realm of the shadow puppets.

Located on the corner of Great Jones and Bowery Streets in Manhattan's lower east side, the Great Jones Shadow Puppet Theater houses performance space for traditional and non-traditional Javanese shadow puppet shows, or *Wayang Kulit*. The stage is located at roof-level on top of commercial and manu-facturing space. Thus, the audience member's journey to the theater is elongated to allow the reality of the city to fade before entering the performance space.

The path to the stage is carved out of the building's mass. One passes under and back through a thickened outer wall. The thickness of the building's walls is juxtaposed with the seeming thinness of the shadow puppet screen. The screen in one sense has immeasurable thickness as it holds the histories and the imagi-nation of the Javanese peoples. In the end, the Shadow Puppet Theater attempts to convey the limitless space of the imagination.

Advisor

Darell Fields

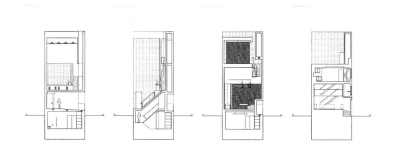

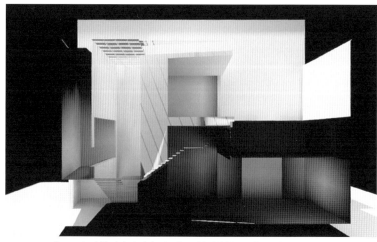

Conceptual Model: Jack in the Box, Model Views, Cross Sections moving through Building East to West, and Longitudinal Section showing Light and Shadow at noon

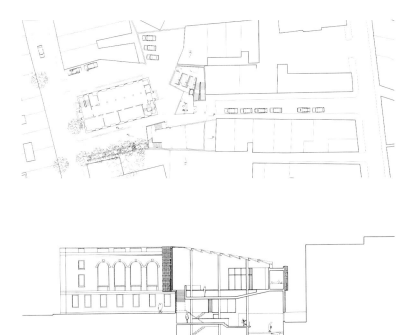

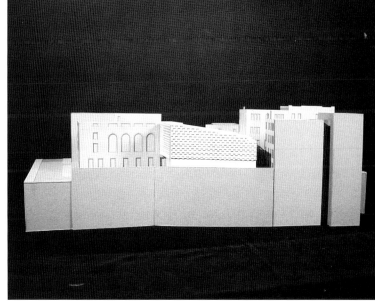

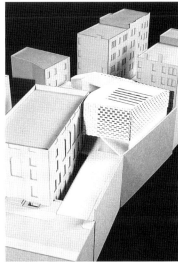

Model View, Ground Floor Plan, Section, Perspective View, and Model Views

Michelle Tarsney
MArch I

bath

The open or ambiguous work does not allow a privileged, definitive, frontal view; rather it encourages the spectator to shift his position continuously in order to see the work in new aspects, as if it were in a state of perpetual transformation. Ambiguity is not vagueness; it is not lacking in definite shape or form. Rather, it allows for a multiplicity of interpretations or readings requiring the discernment of the individual.

My interest in ambiguity stems from Robert Venturi's discussion of it in *Complexity and Contradiction in Architecture*. Venturi refers to William Empson, who cites ambiguity as one of the chief virtues of poetry, where rhyme, alliteration, and rhythm lend additional meaning to the poem. It is this type of perceptual ambiguity that I explored in architectural terms in this thesis.

The vehicle for the investigation was a public bath in the North End of Boston. At the urban scale, the bath operates as both object and context, as field and ground. It reconfigures an existing passageway, allowing the bath to be interpreted as both an addition to the existing Knights of Columbus building and as an autonomous piece. Internally, the narrative or ritual of the bath requires a continuity of space that is in contradiction to the needs for privacy and thermal requirements.

The negotiation between programmatic elements and the sequence of the bathing ritual is articulated through differentiation of materials, changes in lighting, and spatial enclosure, or perceived enclosure. Additionally, changes in movement and in body position allow for varying degrees of private space within a larger public space.

Advisor
Hashim Sarkis

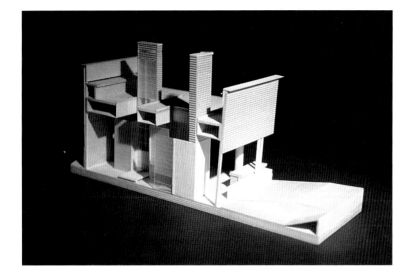

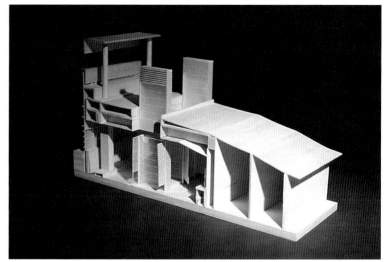

Ming-Yuan Wang
MArch I

Dissolution—The Bathroom Design of New Park in Taipei

Even as homosexuals have emerged in new social spaces in Taiwan in the 1990s, the Taipei city government decided to reinvent Taipei's New Park—a gay meeting area—as a space free of gays through a redesign plan.

This move is the latest in a historical continuum of state efforts to "reform" the park through physical interventions that manipulate its uses and the meanings it holds for people. The Japanese did this when they replaced a Ching Dynasty temple with a monumental governmental building to identify the space as a celebration of Japanese imperial power. The KMT reformed the New Park as the symbolic center of the Chinese nation in exile by building a traditional Chinese pavilion in the park. Today, the Taipei government is identifying the space as queer-free heterosexual space.

In this project, I reassert the New Park's queer significance by inserting and reconstructing a new infrastructure in the form of two different types of public bathrooms. During the day, the bathrooms are individual, heterosexual spaces; at night, they are transformed into a queer, smooth spaces. The transformation is dependent upon the materials. During the day, a two-way mirror is used to make the walls opaque from the outside, but provide a clear view looking out through them to the park. At night, this relationship reverses itself: additional two-way mirrors divide the stalls that segregate genders during the day, and combine them into one unisex bathroom at night. These bathrooms become monuments to homosexuality as it tries to escape from repressive social norms and fights for its right to exist. The constant that ties the park's previous interventions is the repeated layering of meaning on this public space by a succession of political regimes which have struggled to resignify this space. Whereas the previous interventions celebrated cultural icons backed by the state and the dominant culture, this project inscribes the existence of an oppressed and peripheral culture.

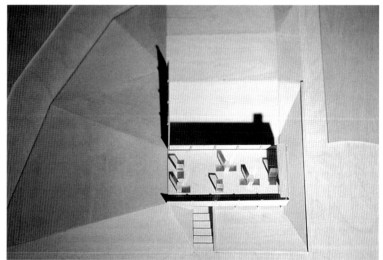

Model Views

Advisor
Darell Fields

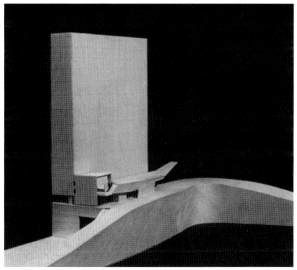

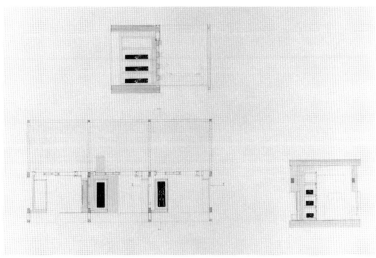

Panorama and Plan of Queens, Section through Mausoleum,
Mausoleum Plans and Sections, and Model View

Wendy Ellen Weintraub
MArch I

Death As A Marker

Sited in New York City between Franklin Delano Roosevelt Drive, the Queensborough Bridge, a heliport landing pad, and the East River, stands the vertical cemetery: a moment of silence amidst the noise of the city. The form reads like an urban-scale headstone along the river's skyline. Its only fenestrated facade is a curtain-wall affording views of the river and park beyond, as well as allowing the wind to pass freely through the mausoleums. This exterior building, a flat cemetery raised up on its end, accommodates the only possible direction for Manhattan's future growth.

Advisor
Darell Fields

Dean Joseph Hudnut
Hugh Stubbins

Prof. Marcel Breuer

Eileen Pei

Costume Ball, ca. 1944.
(Special Collections
Accession M-9)

an Underwood

Franzjiska Porges

Beate Gropius
F. Bruck

J. M. Pei

Warren Radford

B. Nikrodhananda

Alice Wilson

Mary Silver Smith

J. Black

Jean League

**Faculty of Design
1997–1998**

Peter G. Rowe
*Dean, Faculty of Design
Raymond Garbe Professor of
Architecture and Urban Design*

ARCHITECTURE

Emeriti

Gerhard Michael Kallmann
Professor of Architecture Emeritus

Eduard F. Sekler
*Professor of Architecture Emeritus
Osgood Hooker Professor of Visual
Arts Emeritus*

Jerzy Soltan
*Nelson Robinson, Jr., Professor of
Architecture and Urban Design
Emeritus*

Albort Szabo
*Professor of Architecture Emeritus
Osgood Hooker Professor of Visual
Arts Emeritus*

Academic and Adjunct Faculty

D. Michelle Addington
Assistant Professor of Architecture

George Baird
*G. Ware Travelstead Professor of
Architecture*

Carol J. Burns
Associate Professor of Architecture

Howard Burns
*Senior Lecturer in the History of
Architecture*

Preston Scott Cohen
Associate Professor of Architecture

Darell W. Fields
Associate Professor of Architecture

K. Michael Hays
Professor of Architectural Theory

Jacques Herzog
*Arthur Rotch Design Critic in
Architecture*

Kenneth Kao
Lecturer in Architecture

Sheila Kennedy
Associate Professor of Architecture

Rem Koolhaas
*Professor in Practice of Architecture
and Urban Design*

Sarah Williams Ksiazek
*Assistant Professor of Architectural
History*

Jude LeBlanc
Associate Professor of Architecture

William J. LeMessurier
*Adjunct Professor of Architectural
Technology*

Jonathan Levi
Design Critic in Architecture

George Liaropoulos-Legendre
Assistant Professor of Architecture

Malcolm M. McCullough
Associate Professor of Architecture

Pierre de Meuron
*Arthur Rotch Design Critic in
Architecture*

Enric Miralles
Design Critic in Architecture

José Rafael Moneo
*Josep Lluis Sert Professor of
Architecture*

Toshiko Mori
Professor in Practice of Architecture

João António Mota
Lecturer in Architecture

Linda Pollak
Design Critic in Architecture

Spiro N. Pollalis
*Professor of Design Technology and
Management*

Monica Ponce de Leon
Assistant Professor of Architecture

Luis Rojo de Castro
Design Critic in Architecture

Peter Rose
Adjunct Professor of Architecture

Carl M. Sapers
*Adjunct Professor of Studies in
Professional Practice in Architecture*

Antoine Hashim Sarkis
Assistant Professor of Architecture

Daniel L. Schodek
*Kumagai Professor of Architectural
Technology*

Mack Scogin
*Kajima Adjunct Professor of
Architecture*

Jorge Silvetti
*Nelson Robinson, Jr., Professor of
Architecture*

Christine Smith
*Robert C. and Marian K. Weinberg
Professor of Architectural History*

Wilfried Wang
Adjunct Professor of Architecture

Val K. Warke
Lecturer in Architecture

James Williamson
Assistant Professor of Architecture

T. Kelly Wilson
Assistant Professor of Architecture

Visiting Faculty

Alex Anmahian
Rocco Ceo
Ned Collier
Jan Olav Jensen
Carlos Jimenez
Silvia Kolbowski
Vittorio Lampugnani
Francisco Liernur
Tim Love
Francisco Mangado
Sandro Marpillero
Detlef Mertins
Daniel Monk
Mark Mulligan
Paul Wesley Nakazawa
Charles Rose
Nigel Smith
Maryann Thompson
Calvin Tsao
Mirko Zardini

LANDSCAPE ARCHITECTURE

Emeriti

Charles Ward Harris
Professor of Landscape Architecture Emeritus

Frederick Edward Smith
Professor of Advanced Environmental Studies in Resources and Ecology Emeritus

Academic and Adjunct Faculty

John Beardsley
Senior Lecturer in Landscape Architecture

Miroslava Marie Beneš
Associate Professor of the History of Landscape Architecture

Anita Berrizbeitia
Assistant Professor of Landscape Architecture

Phillip J. Craul
Senior Lecturer in Landscape Architecture

Peter Del Tredici
Lecturer in Landscape Architecture

Joseph Disponzio
Assistant Professor of Landscape Architecture

Richard T. T. Forman
Professor of Advanced Environmental Studies in the Field of Landscape Ecology

Robert L. France
Assistant Professor of Landscape Ecology

George Hargreaves
Professor in Practice of Landscape Architecture

Gary R. Hilderbrand
Assistant Professor of Landscape Architecture

Niall G. Kirkwood
Associate Professor of Landscape Architecture

Anne Scott McGhee
Lecturer in Landscape Architecture

Martha Schwartz
Adjunct Professor of Landscape Architecture

Kenneth W. Smith
Design Critic in Landscape Architecture

Carl F. Steinitz
Alexander and Victoria Wiley Professor of Landscape Architecture and Planning

John R. Stilgoe
Robert and Lois Orchard Professor in the History of Landscape Development

Rossana Vaccarino
Assistant Professor of Landscape Architecture

Michael R. Van Valkenburgh
Charles Eliot Professor in Practice of Landscape Architecture

Visiting Faculty

Michael Blier
Holly Getch Clarke
Hope Hasbrouck
Elizabeth Dean Hermann
Mark Johnson
Mark Klopfer
Leonard Newcomb
Jacques Simon
Laura Solano
Marc Treib
Matthew Urbanski

URBAN PLANNING AND DESIGN

Emeriti

William A. Doebele
Frank Backus Williams Professor of Urban Planning and Design Emeritus

Gerald M. McCue
John T. Dunlop Professor of Housing Studies Emeritus

Academic and Adjunct Faculty

Alan A. Altshuler
Ruth and Frank Stanton Professor in Urban Policy and Planning

J. Miller Blew III
Adjunct Professor of Real Estate Development

Leland D. Cott
Design Critic in Urban Planning and Design

Rodolphe el-Khoury
Assistant Professor of Urban Planning and Design

José A. Gomez-Ibañez
Derek C. Bok Professor of Urban Planning and Public Policy

Jerold S. Kayden
Associate Professor of Urban Planning

Alex Krieger
Professor in Practice of Urban Design

M. David Lee
Adjunct Professor of Urban Planning and Design

Rodolfo Machado
Professor in Practice of Architecture and Urban Design

Martha Ann O'Mara
Assistant Professor of Real Estate Development in the Fields of Management and Organizational Behavior

Edward Robbins
Lecturer in Urban Design

Peter G. Rowe
Raymond Garbe Professor of Architecture and Urban Design

Mona A. Serageldin
Adjunct Professor of Urban Planning

Julia Trilling
Assistant Professor of Urban Planning

François C. D. Vigier
Charles Dyer Norton Professor of Regional Planning

Visiting Faculty

Doris Behrens-Abouseif
Jean-Pierre Buffi
Joan Busquets
Richard Dimino
Douglas Dolezal
John Driscoll
Kathryn Firth
Alexander von Hoffman
James Kostaras
Scott Levitan
David Listokin
Rebecca Robertson
Barry Shaw
Sarah Whiting
Robert Yaro

Credits

Dean, Faculty of Design
Peter G. Rowe

Director of Lectures, Exhibitions,
and Academic Publications
Brooke Hodge

Graphic Design and
Project Coordination
Margaret L. Fletcher

Project Assistance
Michelle Fuson

Model Photography
Pavlina Lucas, Boston

Flat Photography
Anita Kan, Cambridge
Spectrum Select Imaging, Boston
Typotech, Cambridge

Production Assistance
Chantelle Brewer
Rami el-Samahy
Jeannie Kim

Printing
Bolger Publications/Creative Printing,
Minneapolis, MN

Photography Credits
Pages 6, 8, Anita Kan

Pages 12, 14–29, 60–75, 106–109,
144–161, 180–181, John F. Cook

Page 1, "Water Gropius with Cigar,"
Process Architecture Publishing Company

Pages 2–3, "John Brinckerhoff Jackson,"
A Sense of Place, A Sense of Time, ed. by
Eleanor McPeck, Municipal Art Society, NY,
NY, 1996, photograph by Douglas Merriam

Page 5, "Josep Lluis Sert," Courtesy of the
Frances Loeb Library, Graduate School of
Design, Harvard University

Pages 28–29, 74–75, Anderson, E.;
Davis, C.; Oskula, J.; and Whitney,
G. ROBINSON HALL. [ca. 197–?]
(Sekler Student Report, #259)

Pages 106–107, LeBoutillier, George T.
GSD 40 Notebooks (Special
Collections Accession M–11)

Page 108, *TASK, A MAGAZINE FOR THE
YOUNGER GENERATION IN ARCHITECTURE.*
Cambridge, 1941–1948. (Rare Periodical)

Pages 160–161, Harvard University.
Graduate School of Design. [Papers concerning the School's involvement in the
events of April 1969] (Rare Ref H261n)

Archival material courtesy of the
Special Collections Department, Frances
Loeb Library, Graduate School of Design,
Harvard University.

*Special thanks to Mary Daniels and Lisa
Starzyk-Weldon (Special Collections) and
Alix Reiskind (Visual Resources) of the
Frances Loeb Library for their advice and
assistance with the archival material.*